Motivation for Learning

Motivation for Learning

A Guide for the Teacher of the Young Adult

Stanford C. Ericksen

Ann Arbor
The University of Michigan Press

To Susanna, Eugene, Stanford, Jr., and David

Preface

This book is written for teachers, parents, and administrators as an account of how students learn and what can be done to improve the conditions for acquiring knowledge and forming new attitudes and values. It is not a how-to-do-it manual, nor a super-synthesis of different theories of learning. What I want to do is describe the main ideas about motivation and learning that are prerequisite for good teaching in most content-specific courses.

For the past twelve years my professional effort has been almost totally linked to the research and service program at the Center for Research on Learning and Teaching at the University of Michigan. In this work we have found that teachers are more likely to introduce needed changes if they understand the ideas that justify and support the different techniques and climates for instruction. I have tried, therefore, to transform the findings and principles from research and theory on motivation, learning, thinking, social psychology, and personality development into the practical procedures of teaching a course. I have assumed that the teacher is less interested in learning about psychology than in improving his or her impact on students as individual persons.

It is not presumed that college students are qualitatively different from those in high school. Education is becoming more flexible at both levels as the traditional "square" classroom gives way to a variety of instructional arrangements. In any case, projecting one's voice to the back of the room and projecting visual images to the front are judged to be less important for teaching than is the instructor's ability to make sense to young adults, to challenge their curiosity, and to provide the resources for learning.

The question is constantly before us at the Center: how can a relatively small research and service unit influence the teaching practices of a large university? One answer has been the publication of our *Memo to the Faculty* series which reports new developments related to teaching. I have drawn freely from these *Memos* for substantive material, and most of the examples come from the work of the Center with teachers on our own campus.

I am, of course, deeply indebted to the influence of my past and present associates at the Center: Donald R. Brown, Wayne K. Davis, George L. Geis, James M. Hedegard, Frank M. Koen, James A. Kulik, Wilbert J. McKeachie, Jean B. Mann, Patricia O'Connor, Hazen J. Schumacher, Jr., David D. Starks, and Karl L. Zinn. Our staff meetings, project conferences, and informal day-to-day discussions have shaped my opinions although I must accept full responsibility for errors, false generalizations, and misplaced applications. Special recognition must be given to Barbara Z. Bluestone for her excellent editorial critiques of my *Memo* manuscripts and the earlier drafts of the chapters in this book.

Chapters 1, 2, 5, 6, 8, and 9 are essentially original although certain headings and phrasing have been carried over from some of my other publications, talks, and convention papers. Chapters 3, 4, and 7 are extensions of my *Memos* on "Learning Theory and the Teacher" and much of the material in Chapters 10 (with Steve Riskind), 11, 12, and 13 first appeared as a *Memo*.

Contents

Chapter 1

The Student as an Individual

We need new words for "teaching"; words that say more about why and how a student learns and remembers, how his attitudes change and his values take shape. The conventional vocabulary favors talk about different styles of teaching, about methods of communication, curricular reform, and instructional innovation. Questions about what is best for students are answered only indirectly and by implication. The new language about teaching must offer greater detail about the conditions for learning: how ambitions are stirred; how some anxieties are lessened and new ones generated; how the store of information in memory grows; by what process old labels acquire new meaning; how abstract concepts are formed, generalizations tested, and value judgments explored; how attitudes are sharpened as new knowledge is examined and combined with what the student already knows. Finally, the language of teaching must deal with the processes the student uses to clarify his own picture of who he is, what he is doing, and where he is going—solo and as a member of society.

College teaching has never been more challenging or rewarding—when successful. Students are critical judges and their standards are valid: they don't want to waste educational time or to be overlooked as individuals. Although good teaching takes many forms, the most important resources for its success are carried by the students when they walk into the classroom. This book seeks to examine how the teacher can utilize these interests and talents for the acquisition of knowledge.

The Individual Student as the Moving Force for Educational Change

Higher education relaxed too soon in believing it no longer needed to prove itself. Its leaders learned how to find and to spend research money and how to run nationwide consulting agencies. They discovered that time and money could be saved through mass teaching, and with tighter budgets, the pressure mounts for the faculty to increase "productivity" by teaching more students. But simply exposing students to knowledge is an educationally defeating response to the budget squeeze. Other methods of instruction must be found that will improve the conditions for learning without compromising the flexibility and diversity of education, and this may be the main education challenge for the rest of this decade.

The individual student brings with him distinctive resources for transforming what he studies into knowledge with personal meaning. Under any instructional arrangement, the student will learn best what he perceives as worth learning. In a class of 5, 50, or 500, each student listens selectively, generates distinctive associations, speculates in his own cognitive style about what he hears, and draws his own inferences and generalizations. Each student remembers, forgets, and amalgamates selective items of information in unique combinations. Regardless of how he is taught, he learns in his own distinctive style. The student, not the class, is the de facto unit of instruction. A number of obstacles obscure this fact: the anonymity of numbers as enrollments level out and as teaching loads go up, the pressures of nonteaching demands, and the sometimes indifferent attitudes of students themselves. The path of least resistance is to fit students into an efficient system of instruction organized around uniform bodies of knowledge. But standardized mass production does not lead to efficiency in education as it does in industry. Howard R. Bowen (1972), an economist, teacher, and administrator, provides a good perspective on the problem:

> Efficiency in higher education remains a complex matter. Society may be in danger of trying to restrict the functions of higher education too narrowly and to convert institutions into mere assembly lines generating credit hours, rather than allowing them to function as centers of learning and culture. It would be a mistake, harmful both to education and to social welfare, to turn colleges and universities into credit-and-degree manufacturers and to judge them solely by their productivity in these terms . . . Good education requires a spirit of inquiry, a center of culture, and contact with intellectual and social problems. (p. 199)

External demands for conformity, uniformity, and standardization haunt the intrinsic diversity of a good university. Certain academic values stand out and are worth defending, for both teachers and students. Freedom for self-analysis is one. Freedom to search for objective truth is another. Freedom of inquiry—inward or outward—is the primary value; the history of higher education is essentially the history of learning how to protect and utilize freedom of inquiry, whether to satisfy pure curiosity, to solve a current problem, or to look ahead of the generation ahead. It is the principle that allows an institution to question its own orthodoxy as well as to examine openly the state of knowledge, the state of society, and the state of the interchange between the two. Open inquiry is meaningless, however, if the pressure for conformity restrains students from freely using their individual talents to search and to understand new ideas. The student learns best when he can exercise control over his own mental processes. The primary task of the teacher is to set the stage for individual thinking and to support its direction and redirection.

The Learning Model

The findings of research on human learning give the teacher solid information with which to plan the instructional arrangements for his course of study. "The learning model" for education stresses the conditions for learning; how the teacher influences what students learn and think about; how they feel; and what they do now and after leaving the classroom. Three major tasks confronting the teacher are derived from the learning model:

1. The teacher makes decisions about course objectives and the organization of content material. Books and machines can present information, peers can motivate (as can learning itself), but the teacher, the subject-matter specialist, must take the lead in defining course content. These decisions take into account not only the "hard" facts, concepts, and methods of his field, but also the concerns of his students.

2. The teacher's presence in the classroom is

especially important as he establishes the climate of the class and influences the level of student expectation. It is in this central teaching role that he provides the internal consistency among his three tasks.

3. Evaluation is the third dimension of the teacher's role. It is not his exclusive responsibility, however, since students continuously evaluate their own performances. Criteria for evaluating student achievement can be objective and clearly observable, or they can be fuzzy and difficult to define. Teaching is made easier when objective criteria for intellectual achievement are available but these measures, such as how well students memorize minutiae, may not always be as educationally worthwhile as are the more subtle indicators of attitude and value changes.

"Bright" Students and Other Individual Differences

The learning model sets the student forth in bold relief. He is the source of the more significant factors that determine the rate, the direction, and level of academic performance. Most attention has been given to scholastic aptitude—how bright are our students? We live in a test-dominated society, and the tenacious fixation on the bright student has become one of the more restricting features of higher education. Test-taking intelligence is, of course, a valuable asset and numerous research studies show this factor to be the single most significant measured variable in academic achievement. Nevertheless, we must relax our dogged adherence to scholastic aptitude and achievement measures, and to grade-point averages as the means of defining and evaluating successful academic performance. Even for students who have been on the college-bound track for most of their lives, scholastic-aptitude tests take account of only about 25 percent of the factors that predict a student's ability to earn good grades during the first two years of college. This is not a particularly impressive relationship but it has, nevertheless, tended to obscure the other student-linked resources that lead to academic success.

The obvious question is what are these other factors and which are most important? To answer in terms of categories, one would immediately point to factors such as motivation to learn, habits of study, positive and negative attitudes, background experiences, and aspirations and ambitions. These are some of the clusters of student-based resources for learning that must be utilized in the course of instruction. Teaching is complicated by the inevitable differences between students; in the distinctive ways, for example, they respond to the nature of what is to be learned, to the climate of the classroom, and to the criteria for evaluating performance.

Lip service has long been given to individual differences, but in practice, educators have used these measured differences to establish cut-off points for admission, special curricular tracks, homogeneous groups, and quantitative criteria of achievement. Educational management has tended to deal with one variable at a time—age, intelligence, achievement measures, completion of prerequisite courses, stated vocational objective, and the like. This kind of sorting and "tracking" obscures the effects of other important variables which interact with one another, as when, for example, a bright student, placed in an "honors" class, becomes overly anxious because he realizes that he may not achieve top status. Some students perform best with an "authoritarian" teacher, whereas other and equally bright students do better with a "permissive" teacher. In any case, good teaching requires that adjustment be made to the interaction between characteristics of the individual student and the variety of conditions in the learning environment.

The psychological inventory of talents, skills, information, interests, needs, and educational goals is unique for each student. Each has particular habits of study, approaches to problem solving, and style of thinking. Every student ". . . step(s) to the music which he hears . . ." and reacts differentially to the influence of his peers, to the personality of his teachers, to specific techniques of teaching, to the use of different media, to the material being learned, and to the prevailing climate of the classroom. Students resent and resist the impersonality that results when short shrift is given to these subtle individual differences.

The research evidence on interaction effects is not, however, overwhelming in its support. These studies usually involve the statistical analysis of large numbers of students, with measuring instruments that fall short of assessing the distinctive, in-depth reactions of the individual student. Nevertheless, when learning ability is viewed in the larger perspective, involving the motivational and personality characteristics of the learner, it is clear that the most significant instructional changes will be those that tap and challenge the unique combination of talents of the individual student:

> The traditional formulations of the nature of individual differences in learning and the traditional modes of education fail to provide enough freedom for the exercise of individual talents. We admire individual performance, but we must do more than merely stand in admiration; we must design the effective conditions under which individuals are provided with the

opportunities and rewards to perform at their best and in their own way. (Robert Glaser, 1972, p. 12)

The Zigzag Curve of Learning

Slowly, education is beginning to recognize the individual student as the central unit of instruction. Other professions have been more aggressive than educators in developing their services to meet the needs of individuals. The uncompromising responsibility of the law, for example, is to protect the rights and freedom of the individual citizen, and medicine places great value on the personal doctor-patient relationship. The library sets a good example for the faculty since it is maintained as an education resource to serve the individual purposes of students and teachers. Its high cost could be drastically reduced if it were to trade off individual accommodation in favor of production-line service for high demand use only. Personal, educational, and vocational counseling calls for individual attention. But why is it that arrangements for supporting learning and thinking have remained, for the most part, in the mass mode?

The theories and principles of learning are described by the learning researcher in the generalized abstract language of science—the smooth-function curves of learning that represent the progress of learners in general but no student in particular. Likewise, educational research has too long stayed comfortably in line with the conventions of educational mass production. More often than not, the "class" has been the unit of study as investigators tested ways of raising the performance average for the group. In contrast, we would like to think of the teacher as being concerned with particular students and with the unpredictable zigs and zags that each student makes through the abstract, theoretical curve of learning.

Offering educational freedom to the individual student is *not* giving him license to do what he pleases and when. A college student is a participating member of an educational institution, and the goals he seeks must necessarily be consistent with the objectives and resources available at his school. These differ markedly from one school to another and the prospective student should know what these are and how they might effect his own educational plan. James Kulik (1973) described two extremes in department-level adaptations to individual instruction—one via a thoroughly humanistic climate and the other via a thoroughly behavioristic climate.

In the Psychology Department at Sonoma State College in California, personal relevance dominates decisions as to the course of instruction. For example, three courses in Asian psychology were being given, covering, respectively, I Ching, Yoga, and Zen. Seminars on Man and Woman, Self-Emerging, Nonviolence, Death and Dying, and so on "appear to be the backbone of the program" (p. 140). Students are encouraged to maintain journals of one's experiences, reactions, and impressions; dyads are formed and considerable attention is given to nonverbal communication. There can be little doubt that this is a successful program in terms of its popularity. "No other school in the country has as high a percentage of psychology majors" (p. 147).

The contrasting institution drawn from Kulik's survey of departments of psychology is Western Michigan University in Kalamazoo. A visitor first notices the bulletin boards that line the corridor on which are neatly stapled grade sheets and cumulative graphs charting students' progress in the beginning course. A student sits beside a Plexiglas box that encases a pigeon in a "reinforcement" demonstration. "Off the main corridor is a room divided by partitions painted in psychedelic designs where undergraduate students consult with other undergraduates— their teaching assistants, tutors, course administrators. Another classroom is furnished with numerous small tables for four-man discussion groups . . ." (p. 116).

The distinctive curricular features are: (1) The core courses are sequenced in a linear manner, (2) behavioristic content is emphasized, (3) positive reinforcement is the significant common denominator of teaching practices, (4) provision is made for apprenticeship experiences in teaching, research, and behavior modification projects.

These two schools may be "overboard" applications of good intentions but prototype examples of doctrinaire-based innovations serve a very useful purpose. In the end, however, the changes necessary to support independent learning must be made by individual teachers and for particular courses. Perhaps the most active single type of instructional redesign throughout the country is in the direction of self-paced progress toward prescribed curricular goals.

No teacher, however, can be all things to all students and so responsibility for matching means with ends rests ultimately with each student. He must be his own best critic even though, in most instances, the precollege experiences have taught him to lean on the teacher rather than to gain the assurance and the capabilities of a self-directed program of study. These abilities for independent learning are underused when students are required to move lockstep through the established curricular requirements.

When the class hour is ended and the student walks away, what happens to all the instructor has said and done? The teacher has carefully defined and organized the objectives of the course in a logical sequence, maintained a constructive environment for learning in the classroom, and made his evaluations promptly, fairly, and in detail. The student then proceeds to do what only he can do, namely, to integrate what he has been taught by the instructor with what he has learned elsewhere. As he sharpens and shapes his own educational purposes, new combinations of ideas are added to what he already knows. The maturation of each student's private knowledge continues as he studies other subjects, and as he lives and learns away from the classroom.

The irrelevancies and peripheral items gradually fade and settle down out of the way. From one term to the next the student improves his ability to structure his own thinking as necessary to achieve his own education objectives. A teacher's best contribution to a student's education is to help him learn how to learn independently. Higher education has not yet fully realized the intellectual and personal power of the individual student who has been given a chance to progress at his own pace and within his own style of learning and thinking.

Chapter 2

The Theory of the Learner

"Learning theory" is a catch-all phrase but is basic to education nonetheless. In its narrow sense, learning theory offers a pinpoint analysis of such specific processes as eye-blink conditioning, rote memorizing, or concept formation. In its broader use, it becomes interchangeable with "behavior theory." The researcher in this field analyzes and describes the nature of learning in general and gives only passing thought to how abstract conceptions might be used in a prescriptive way in the classroom. As one highly productive learning theorist acknowledged, his research had ". . . little or nothing to do with learning in real life situations, including even the kinds of learning that are supposed to go on in the schoolroom" (Spence, 1959, p. 84). Information about how students learn does not come off the learning theory shelf as neatly packaged principles ready for application. Theory provides background information about the basic nature of the different learning processes; a guide for decision-making, and a perspective for passing judgment on the constant parade of "innovative" arrangements for teaching that often border on educational quackery.

The Nature of Formal Learning Theory

Many different theories of human learning have been formulated but all make their start from a particular dimension of human experience—as does philosophy, literature, or theology—and then proceed to work out an internally consistent explanation. Most formal theories begin as a "revolt" from some other theory or point of view and quickly develop a characteristic set of concepts which sharpens the contrast between one theory and another. With further empirical research, debate, and application, however, the differences become softened. The synthesis moves research closer to a more balanced analysis of the way students learn—how complex individuals acquire command over complex bodies of knowledge and a sense of their meaning.

Behaviorism: Learning by Association

In simplest terms, the association theories view learning as a process of connecting, of establishing a bond between movement, sensation, and ideas. Aristotle stated this principle in his explanation of "recollection":

> . . . when one wishes to recollect, this is what he will do: he will try to obtain a beginning of movement whose sequel shall be the movement which he desires to reawaken. This explains why attempts at recollection succeed soonest and best when they start from a beginning. For, in order of succession, the mnemonic movements are to one another as the objective facts. Accordingly, things arranged in the fixed order, like the successive demonstrations in geometry, are easy to remember, while badly arranged subjects are remembered with difficulty. (Ross, 1927, pp. 217–18)

The revival of the learning-by-association point of view was made by the British Empiricists. In 1690 John Locke's *An Essay Concerning Human Understanding* postulated that complex ideas result from the creative combination (association) of simple or unanalyzed ideas. Successive philosophers in the British Empirical school developed the association concept in greater detail and derived the principle of *contiguity* as the primary law of association; an association is formed between two events when they are experienced simultaneously or in immediate succession. During the past fifty years behavioristic theories of learning have used learning-by-association as the integrating principle.

The conditioned response. Ivan P. Pavlov (1849–1936) developed the basic technique of the conditioned response. He was interested in neurological, not psychological, problems and showed little interest in the experimental applications of his techniques by American investigators in their studies on learning. Basically, the Pavlovian conditioning paradigm consists of pairing a new stimulus (a tone) with a familiar stimulus (food) which produces a particular response (salivation). After repeated pairings, the tone will elicit salivation in the absence of the food itself. Something new has been added to the dog's repertoire of responses; he has *learned* to salivate to the auditory signal. The salivating dog became the symbol, if not the prototype, of how conditioning is presumed to account for learning in general. According to conditioned response theory, any stimulus can be "conditioned" to produce responses not normally associated with that stimulus. Learning is the process of conditioning a stimulus to a response.

John B. Watson (1878–1958) founded Behaviorism as an extension of the Pavlovian paradigm. Conditioning, he believed, was controlled by the contiguous (together in time) association between stimulus and response. Watson claimed, for example, that a normal child could be trained to achieve almost any vocational role by means of a sequential chain of S-R (stimulus-response) conditioning. Behaviorism was presented as the new science for the direction and the control of human thoughts, feelings, and action—the behavioral technology for a "Brave New World" and other conceptions of the controlled society.

Trial and error learning. Edward L. Thorndike (1874–1949) developed his theory of learning, the Law of Effect, from experiments in trial-and-error learning rather than from conceptions of the conditioned response. The learner is rewarded or punished depending upon what he does; the "effect" (satisfaction or annoyance) is contingent upon how the learner responds to the environment. Thorndike observed, for example, that a cat trying to escape from a puzzle box would make many different kinds of responses—pushing, squeezing, scratching, biting and, finally, pulling the string that opened the door. Responses that did not further the cat's escape from the box were "stamped out" over a number of trials, and responses that led to success were "stamped in." Later experiments with humans confirmed his belief that rewarding a response strengthens learning and retention more effectively than does mere repetition (drill).

Conditioning by reinforcement. Clark L. Hull (1884–1952) followed Thorndike as the most powerful single voice in learning theory. Hull accepted the Law of Effect in principle and merged this basic explanatory thesis into a far-ranging, systematic theory of behavior. His theory of learning, like Watson's, was stated in terms of conditioning between stimulus and response, but Hull went further than raw empiricism and drew inferences about processes going on *within* the learning organism. The weight of his argument rested on the idea of "drive reduction": reinforcing effects are derived directly and solely from the motivational state of the learner. Food is reinforcing to a hungry rat but not to a thirsty animal; a good grade is reinforcing to a scholarship candidate but is a matter of less moment to a student whose educational goals are inner-directed. The rate of learning is determined by the strength of the motivation, the magnitude of the reward, and the elapsed time between reward (drive reduction) and response. Hull's theory has significant implications for teaching: motivation precedes learning, and learning itself requires reinforcement (feedback, knowledge of results) from the covert or overt responses made by the learner.

The "contingencies of reinforcement" is the main integrating principle in the analysis of behavior by B. F. Skinner (1904–   ). He bypassed the inferential constructs of a formal *theory* of learning by stressing the empirical relations between reinforcement and behavior change. He transformed Behaviorism into a behavioral technology (*The Technology of Teaching*, 1968). Because of its widespread influence on contemporary education, this point of view is given separate treatment in Chapter 7.

Cognitive Theory

Cognitive theory stems from the Gestalt school of psychology that developed in Germany during and shortly after World War I. Gestalt theory and its derivatives emphasize the *molar* features of experience—the total response of the organism to its environment—in contrast to *molecular* analyses of stimuli and responses. Attention is directed to how the individual perceives the relations between the parts and the whole—the figure to the ground. Experimenters in the cognitive tradition typically arrange rather complex problem tasks and watch their subjects for evidence of insight—the "Eureka" experience.

In cognitive theory, learning consists of developing "expectations," learning what-leads-to-what. Behavior is goal-oriented and learning is essentially the process of building up a "cognitive map"—relationships between cues from the environment and the learner's expectations; the combination of the learner's purposes and his perception of the external field. When a rat successfully runs through a maze, or when a man drives to his office through a maze of city streets, each is performing what has already been learned as a central, brain-map process.

Cognitive theory insists that learning be distinguished from performance. Learning is the central *organization* of mental events (knowledge, cognitions) that can be drawn upon, like money in the bank, when external conditions make it expedient to perform. Learning does not depend on motivation; performance does. Motivation is important primarily as the means of bringing centrally stored information into use. Since instruction is aimed at both the acquisition of knowledge and its use, the teacher must accept responsibility for both learning and performance. Ausubel's concept of "advance organizers" (1968) is a specific instructional application of cognitive theory: the student first studies a relatively short body of material—the organizer—that has been carefully prepared to be at a higher level of abstraction, generality, and inclusiveness than the more factual subject matter later to be learned. For example, an overview of the important principles and concepts of bone structure would help to "organize" the current store of information in the learner's memory in relation to what he is about to learn—the anatomy of the bones of the body. Presumably, the student will be motivated to *perform* well on the test of his knowledge of anatomy.

The terms and concepts of cognitive theory seem to fit in quite naturally with the observations of everyday living, the mental development of the child and the intellectual processes of the adult. For the associationists, the analysis of the "higher mental processes" was almost a side effect to their main interest in the connections between S (stimulus) and R (response). For the Gestalt psychologists, however, concept formation, perceptual meaning, problem solving, and thinking were, themselves, the central concern of research and theory. Cognitive theory is now the reference term for this point of view and, for example, as cognitive psychologists Dennis E. Egan and James G. Greeno (1973) reviewed the current literature on concept learning, serial pattern learning, and problem solving. It is apparent from such analyses that research designed to defend a comprehensive theory of behavior (associative or cognitive) is giving way to the search for information about particular aspects of learning and thinking.

Problem-Oriented Research on Learning

The initial impetus for research on learning (as distinguished from the development of formal theories of learning) came from the "functionalists," with their eclectic but pragmatic analysis of adaptive behavior. These early American psychologists were greatly influenced by the Darwinian biological model and its rejection of the dualism between man and animal. Basically, the subject matter of the discipline of psychology was changed from the analysis of what the mind *is* to the study of what the mind *does*. Rather than being examined as an isolated entity, the mind was considered to be the instrument by which individuals can successfully engage their environment.

John Dewey (1859–1951) was the leader in the development of this new point of view. He insisted that pragmatic criteria be applied to the closed educational system that had long resisted objective evaluation of either its method or its product. Knowledge for its own sake, he believed, was a weak rationale for the curriculum; mental discipline was inadequate as an educational objective, and the mystique of teaching was too far divorced from the conditions necessary for learning by students. Learning became the central theme in American psychology and the groundwork was laid for the experimental analysis of learning and the analytical study of individual differences. These analyses became the scientific basis for new conceptions of what education should accomplish for the individual and for society.

Rather than offering a set of laws to which teaching must conform, problem-oriented learning research is eclectic in theory. This flexibility increases its relevance to college teaching which, because of its range and variety, does not lend itself to a well-ordered, preset system of applications. Certain instances in later chapters will emphasize the *factual findings* from research or the *principles* will be stressed in these applications. A third type of application to teaching can be taken from the *methodology* of research on learning. The procedural ground rules are important in the analysis of learning and some of these carry over to the analysis of instructional support for learning. Three procedural refinements have special importance for guarding against false interpretations of the effects of different modes of teaching:

1. *Independent and dependent variables.* It is always helpful when the teacher can accurately distinguish the primary factors from those having secondary effects on the performance of his students. The nomenclature from experiments on learning is relevant here. The *independent* (x) variable in an experiment is the factor being tested. The *dependent* (y) variable refers to the responses which are directly observed and measured, e.g., the effect of caffeine (independent variable) on ability to recall (dependent variable) a previously memorized list of words.

The same relationship applies to classroom projects on teaching. Loosely speaking, the lecture may be thought of as an independent variable and the test score as the dependent variable. If students who heard the lecture score about the same as those who did not, there may be several explanations, since other factors may obscure the effects of the lecture—the test may be a better measure of the ability to read what is in the textbook than of the ability to understand what was heard from the lecture. It is difficult to isolate independent variables in a complex instructional setting and it is equally difficult to define dependent variables that are valid indicators of the changes in the student that are intended.

Experiments on teaching can also often be faulted for their excessive involvement with variables of secondary importance for learning. As a consequence, most studies that compare one teaching procedure (independent variable) with a "control" conclude with the inconclusive "no significant differences." The task of designing and carrying out a classroom experiment involves an almost infinite universe of variables, singly and in combination, and the teacher/experimenter is usually aware of only a few of these. Some degree of order to this otherwise chaotic state is given by the three categories widely used in learning research: *procedural variables* (class size, teaching style, use of different media); *task variables* (learning facts, concepts, or skills); and *individual difference variables* (motivation, attitudes, intelligence, study habits). This third category includes factors that are usually more important for achievement than are factors from the other two categories. The medium of instruction, for example, turns out to have a less important effect on student performance than improving the internal organization of course content or enabling students to capitalize on the unique talents and interests that they themselves bring into the classroom.

2. *Confounding variables.* Research on learning rarely "discovers" new phenomena; a more likely contribution is to untangle the *confounding* variables. Variables are said to be confounded when the result of an experiment is influenced by two or more factors operating in combination. Many different variables combine in overlapping confusion in the educational setting. Opinion is nearly always divided as to the relative effects of: previous training; the talents, aptitudes, and abilities of students; their interests, motives, attitudes, and values; the instructional impact of the teacher; the influence of the physical environment; the campus traditions and its academic atmosphere. The answer to educational cause and effect is never obvious, and rarely is it agreed upon.

When something unplanned but educationally worthwhile has happened it may be better to leave the variables in their tangled state than to draw erroneous conclusions and misdirected generalizations. A specific instructional innovation may be successful primarily because of its novelty (whether recognized or not)—a visiting speaker, student participation, a new mode of visual projection, a field trip, a new testing or teaching technique. The novelty effect becomes a confounding variable, and its educational impact will gradually weaken as the novelty wears off. Students will usually perceive a special effort on the part of the teacher as showing that he cares and is making a sincere attempt to offer a worthwhile course. In such an instance the effective variable may be the teacher's attitude rather than the experimental feature itself. Examples of this type of constructive educational confounding can be found on nearly every campus and, in the absence of more detailed and specific evidence, may itself be a sufficient reason to encourage educational experimentation and change.

3. *Operationism.* As a method, science speaks about "public information," which it favors, in contrast to "private information," which it distrusts. Research on learning has generally turned to operationism as the best way to make private knowledge public, and then to test its validity. The term signifies that the interpretation of any given observation is limited by the specific procedures—the operations—used to bring about that which is being observed. Operationism acts as a strong deterrent to unrestrained rhetoric and free-wheeling speculation about what goes into the educational process and what comes out, and why.

The educational analyst uses operational definitions to clarify what he is talking about. Chapter 9, for example, is my way of specifying what is meant to "teach students how to think" but the classroom teacher must be even more concrete and "operational" within his content area. What do students mean when they ask for greater relevance? The answer must at least distinguish short- from long-term goals and specifications with respect to self, society, or to the discipline itself. Care must be taken, of course, not to oversimplify these limits, since rigid and narrow operational definitions defeat the original advantage of this procedural constraint. To define intelligence, for example, in terms of "what intelligence tests measure" begs the question.

The Theory of the Learner and the Practice of the Teacher

A few key points in the development of the science of learning and its relevance to teaching have been summarized above. Application is not automatic; the teacher serves as mediator between theory and practice. He must distinguish, for example, between the inferences derived from classical-learning theory and the more pragmatic results of problem-oriented research. And there are other distinctions: molecular analysis in contrast to descriptions of molar units of behavior; substantive findings in contrast to procedural refinements; and finally, fact from fanciful implications and generalizations. The language of learning is a mix of references: to the *kind of material* that is being learned (a second language, chemistry, history, and all the other curricular subsets with which students are familiar); to the *site* where learning takes place (at home, at school, on the job, in the residence halls, or on the bus); to the *inferred processes* of learning (insight, memory, decision-making, creativity, and so forth); to the *equipment and/or proce-*

dures used to study learning (such as computer simulation, maze learning, conditioning, and problem-solving).

Neither psychology nor education has ever had a (successful) Linnaeus and this is probably a good thing, since empirically derived categories and logically organized taxonomies tend to become static and to serve their own ends. The domain of learning, therefore, must be examined in its open-ended variety of forms, and learning theorists would not necessarily be the best teachers even if they were to practice what they teach. Research on learning goes its own, abstract, discipline-oriented way, while the teacher, here and now, tries to improve the conditions under which his students learn. Between theory and practice lies a no-man's-land that needs to be crossed.

Sooner or later, the matter of application resolves itself into finding those conditions most appropriate for a given student. In every profession, the transition from the general to the specific is a complicated step; information must be reshaped and "field tested" before being put to practical use. Clinical medical research usually intervenes between the biological scientist and the practicing physician; engineering development connects pure physical-science theory and technological implementation. The teacher at precollege levels is closely linked to the school of education which seeks to bridge the classroom and the behavioral sciences. The college teacher, however, must usually work without the benefit of a similar mediating agency. Chapter 13 describes the essential features of a training program, but these are uncommon and for the most part the college teacher is a self-taught professional; his advanced training as a graduate student has been almost exclusively limited to his discipline specialty, and he must take the initiative if he wishes to improve his ability as a teacher. This is not necessarily a derelict condition since teachers are quite capable of self-appraisal, of benefiting from the constantly available feedback from students, and from suggestions in the relevant literature. On the basis of what he knows and observes, the teacher generates a conception about each student which guides his decisions about how best to be a teacher for a given student. The perceptive teacher is transforming learning theory into a *theory of the learner*—the independent student as the unit around which education revolves.

Chapter 3

Defining Instructional Objectives

Teaching that is organized around a sequence of objectives makes the most efficient use of the student's talent for learning. Intellectual browsing and pedagogical serendipity have their place, but it is to the advantage of both teacher and student to know where they are heading and to know the criteria for successful achievement. The explicit statement of objectives is the first obligation of the teacher to the student, and their acceptance, rejection, or modification is the first obligation of the student to himself.

Too often course goals are stated in very general terms; it is up to the student "to understand the historical origins of Western democracy" or "to appreciate good literature" or "to grasp the significance of chemistry" or "to learn how to think as a psychologist thinks." These are the "purr" words of academia, and there is little point in bothering with instructional objectives if they are undefined, undefinable, or inaccessible to available means of evaluation. As long as the goals of a course remain vague, such a system remains relatively free from the pressures of accountability.

Committees, Teachers, and Students

Determining what knowledge is worth knowing is not the exclusive bailiwick of the teacher, but no one else is more deeply involved or more aware of the difficulties of defining significant rather than trivial objectives. This point is essential since it is tempting for a curriculum committee, for example, to compromise differences of opinions among its members by organizing a course around hard facts, preestablished units of knowledge, or measurable skills. Performance of this order is easier to assess but education must also include subjective values, the affective, the sensual, and compassion for others and for life as legitimate and necessary objectives, however difficult might be their teaching and their assessment.

A curriculum committee is often the locus of power in deciding the goals of instruction, and this is unfortunate if it reduces the commitment and the zest of the teacher toward expressing and defending views or if it divides his authority from his responsibility. When the teacher himself prescribes the knowledge, skills, and attitudes he believes his students should acquire, he is making the kind of value judgments that are expected in his exercise of academic freedom. His decisions are not, of course, insulated from review and debate with his peers, and certainly not from his students.

Clear and valid statements of curricular objectives require the best talent, if not the prophetic power, of a teacher. It is a more demanding professional task than being a "good teacher" in the narrow, information-giving sense. The teacher should constantly be asking himself: at what time in the future will the relevance of a given fact or procedure, concept or attitude, pass its inflection point and start downhill toward obsolescence? His answer should indicate whether or not such material is worth his students' learning either for its own long-term value or as stepping-stone information.

The goals defined by the teacher and the goals sought by the student are not necessarily congruent, and a student has the right to know what to expect from a course. How much freedom should the student have to modify and change the teacher-based objectives? Extensive student participation with respect to goals may be consistent with the aims of a course in literature, for example, or in a problem-oriented social-science offering. In professional training, where the development of skills and the mastery of a core of technical knowledge is emphasized, this freedom by students to select and choose is more limited. What is to be gained by a debate between an experienced teacher and a naïve student over what should be learned with respect to the technical aspects of surgery, new developments in electrical engineering, or the methodology of survey sampling?

Emphasis on defining objectives in the classroom does not presume that it is the only mechanism for the education of students. Excitement and challenge on the campus as a whole is also important but, in the long run, the quality of education depends primarily on the validity of the objectives for a given course. There are no compensatory mechanisms for what should have been learned but was not.

Taxonomy of Instructional Objectives

The most widely referenced taxonomy for educational goals (Bloom, 1956) details six aspects of the *cognitive* domain: (a) recall and recognition of knowledge, (b) comprehension, (c) application, (d) analysis, (e) synthesis, and (f) evaluation. Of these, the lowest order objective is straight recall or recognition of knowledge, i.e., the student shows that he can repeat facts, use terminology, follow a sequence, define criteria, and state principles, generalizations, and theories. This level of learning is relatively easy to frame as instructional objectives and to test on an examination. The more complex objectives such as analysis, synthesis, and evaluation often tend to be "assumed." A second handbook was published eight years later (Krathwohl *et al.*, 1964) to structure the *affective* domain (interests, attitudes, values) for education. For some teachers these affective and personalistic factors are to be touched with the left hand only, but higher education today is deeply involved with objectives that are far more comprehensive than the acquisition of facts, principles, and theories. The current interest in humanistic education deals mainly with these affective goals of instruction—self-fulfillment, authentic human relations, respect for human dignity, individuality, and the like.

Standing alone, the cognitive/affective categories are too abstract to be much help for the teacher in making an analysis of the substance of a given course. The following descriptive categories, widely used in learning research, are essentially nontechnical, common sense, and general enough to be applicable to most academic departments:

1. *Verbal learning of factual information.* "Facts" have a disconcerting way of becoming "nonfacts" in a short period of time, but are prerequisite, nevertheless, to understanding concepts, principles, and generalizations. Each student's hierarchy of knowledge is based on a factual foundation. From his experience as a scientist and teacher Albert Szent-Gyorgi (1964), the Nobel Laureate in biology, indicates his perception of the place of factual detail:

Science tends to generalize, and generalization means simplification. My own science, biology, is not only very much richer than it was in my student days, but is simpler, too. Then it was horribly complex, being fragmented into a great number of isolated principles. Today these are all fused into one single complex with the atomic model in its center. . . . We, in our teaching, should place more emphasis on generalizations than on details. Of course, details and generalizations must be in a proper balance: generalization can be reached only from details, while it is the generalization which gives value and interest to the detail. (p. 1278)

Meaningfulness is the key variable in learning. Only those items that acquire meaning remain in memory and serve the student over time as he moves from place to place and from problem to problem. In order to find meaning, which is personal and subjective, the student must actively participate in the process of evaluating and integrating the raw facts. Writing a term paper, conducting a special project, or discussing an idea in a group contributes to this process.

2. *The acquisition of performance skill.* Skill learning is less important in liberal arts education than in certain areas of professional training. Nevertheless, skill learning involves many of the same conditions of instruction which result in efficient verbal learning and memory: active participation promotes more rapid learning than does passive observation or listening; writing something down or saying it out loud contributes more to retention of verbal learning than simply listening, just as actually performing a complicated medical prodedure teaches things which no amount of observation can accomplish.

3. *Concept formation.* The capacity of college

students to acquire and to manipulate ideas is a more distinctive talent than their ability to memorize by rote. The correlation between intelligence and memorizing capacity with these students is barely higher than zero. Therefore, to be intellectually "efficient," most college courses should be centered around concepts, principles, generalizations, and other forms of abstract thinking. Learning at this conceptual level is what college students do best.

4. *Method, process, and problem solving.* Considerably more is known about teaching substantive material, whether facts, skills, or concepts, than about teaching problem-solving procedures and research methodology. The methods of science and scholarly research are complex and intellectually demanding; they cannot be "taught" as side effects of a laborious study of literature, an exhaustive analysis of historical documents, or a routine performance of exacting laboratory procedures. Being competent in research methodology means being able to define problems, to generate hypotheses, to test theories, to draw inferences from data, to design experiments, and to formulate generalizations. The competent investigator also knows when to continue and when to alter his tack, and when to admit failure. To state all this as an instructional objective is much easier than it is to demonstrate its achievement. As desirable as it might be, education has not yet learned how to teach a generalized skill of problem solving. In terms of rank-order difficulty of teaching, the facts of biology are easier to organize and present to students than the concepts and theories of biological science. More demanding yet is successful instruction in the methods used by biologists to solve problems, answer questions, and conduct research. Closely related is the problem of how best to teach professional students to

acquire the self-renewing capabilities that will, eventually, help them to forestall informational obsolescence in their area of service.

5. *Changing attitudes and values.* The forgetting curve is steep for most of the substantive information that students learn. Fortunately, affective learning—that is, attitude change, the formation of values, and the acquisition of new and stronger educational motives—has greater staying power and is more readily transferred to situations outside the classroom. But attitudes and value change cannot be taught in the usual direct, prescriptive way. Students are moved toward these objectives more by the example the instructor sets than by his platform "sermons." This does not mean, however, that the teacher should bypass the sensitive task of explicitly stating the attitudes and values he would like to see demonstrated by his students. Because the lines between instruction, indoctrination, propaganda, and brain washing are sometimes blurred, it is all the more important to keep this matter on top of the table via the statement of objectives. Open dialogue about these emotionally toned objectives is the best protection against false accusations of "thought control."

6. *Personal development as an instructional objective.* Personal development of students (as expressed in self-identity, self-fulfillment, self-esteem, and other self-reference terms) is a legitimate instructional objective and one to which teachers can and should contribute. In every course teachers influence the process of personal growth, less, perhaps, by what they say than by the models they present as subject-matter specialists interacting with themselves as citizens. Inevitably, a teacher's priority values will surface and to these his students will respond in a plus or minus direction (rarely neutral). Personal de-

velopment need not be formally stated as an explicit goal since these changes are not measured on the final examination nor, presumably, are they reflected in the course grade. There is the danger, moreover, of using this objective as an excuse for educational permissiveness, intellectual and emotional wandering, and miscellaneous palliatives designed to keep students happy.

Robert MacLeod (1965) made an excellent point on the relation between substantive teaching and the personal growth of the student:

> . . . If by growth we mean the actualization of potential, then the *content* of the study becomes all important. The student grows as a new world is opened to him, a world which invites him to observe and question and evaluate, and the extent of his growth will be measured by the depth and the intensity of his engagement. The teaching that stimulates this kind of growth is unashamedly content centered. (pp. 347–48)

This position does not compromise the essential function of the teacher nor does it lessen the dignity of the student.

Erik Erikson (1963) considers self-identity as emerging from the harmonious balance between the influences of one's parents, teachers, and other important people during the course of reaching for personal maturity. Within this context, Ernest Hilgard (1963) points up a consequent dilemma for the college teacher:

> If we are really helpful in this growth process we find ourselves in the ethical dilemma of either enforcing parental values, and thus playing safe, or taking the risks of permitting experimentation with life experiences through which the new identity will emerge. If our teaching is effective it cannot avoid the awkwardness of being caught in a crossfire at this point,

for we can be neither fully on the side of the parents nor fully on the side of the defiant youth.

Students are aware of this dilemma and watch to see how it is resolved by their different teachers as they stand in the crossfire between generations.

Existential-humanistic philosophy is a strong influence among college students and Abraham Maslow (1971) was one of its more articulate spokesmen:

> What do we mean by the discovery of identity? We mean finding out what your real desires and characteristics are and being able to live in a way that expresses them. You learn to be authentic, to be honest in the sense of allowing your behavior and your speech to be the true and spontaneous expression of your inner feelings. Most of us have learned to avoid authenticity. . . . (p. 183)

> One of the goals of education should be to teach that life is precious. If there were no joy in life, it would not be worth living. Unfortunately, many people never experience joy, those all-too-few moments of total life-affirmation which we call peak-experiences. . . . (p. 187)

The kind of experience Maslow was writing about is not a daily event nor one that can be programmed by the teacher. But the teacher can stifle it by insisting on passive conformity to his course plan. Demands for "relevance" express unstated and sometimes unrecognized impulses for self-development as much as they express the feeling of a need for social reform. The student is not a formless lump of clay waiting to be molded by his teachers. He already has a self-concept, but it is incomplete and he knows it. "Who am I and where am I going?" is, for most students, a more important question than "Who killed Julius Caesar?" or "What is the difference between

Pavlov and Skinner?" Students are looking for new models with which to identify, and they have the opportunity to observe firsthand many of the "identities" that make up a faculty, and some degree of emulation, imitation, or rejection is inevitable during the course of the interaction between the teacher and his many different students.

Exposure or Performance?

The preceding section summarized six different categories that may assist the teacher in marking out instructional goals. The nature of the objectives or the boundary limits for a specialized advanced course will be different from those of a survey course. In any case the teacher is challenged to replace the traditional "sunburn theory" of instruction (exposing students to the light of knowledge) with the far more demanding goal of specifying to students the expected changes in intellectual and personal development upon completion of a course.

The emphasis on the achievement of preset objectives is, of course, basic in the learning model. It is the direct carryover to the classroom of one of the first decisions the research investigator must make when he plans an experiment on learning; namely, whether to use the "trials" or the "performance" criterion for learning. Under the former, learning ends after exposure to a predetermined number of trials. All subjects in the experiment receive the assigned number of trials-to-learn, and progress is measured by average time-per-trial, or number of errors, or correct responses made during the allowed sequence of trials. Most colleges practice the counterpart to the "trials" system: given twelve to sixteen weeks in the term, performance is measured at intermediate time units and by how many correct answers have been given by the time the clock stops the final examination. Fast learning is not a particularly sensible measure of academic progress but has become important because it is a convenient index for the management of large-scale instructional programs.

Under the "performance" criterion, a standard of mastery is set in advance and the trials continue until he achieves satisfactory performance. The translation to classroom practice is simple: accomplishment within the preset time limits of the academic calendar takes second place to the demonstrated achievement of the objectives of the course of study. In a general sense, performance of some kind has usually been the basis for assigning a grade and credits— class attendance, passing examinations, completing papers, solving problems, and the like. The "performance" principle is simply more explicit as to what these criteria are and assigns more weight—perhaps exclusively so—to their achievement in determining grades and credits. This principle is a familiar one in advance placement testing, credit by examination, and in programs of training where students are graduated on a proficiency basis. Self-paced study arrangements, e.g., the Keller Plan, and "contract" teaching and grading, use predefined performance criteria. Even in courses aimed at "self-fulfillment" the teacher should indicate in advance the quality of change in personal development that is expected of the students between the first day of the course and the last. Otherwise, the teacher has set up a criterion-free instructional site where to "do your own thing" is the only rule of educational validity.

Courses Oriented Toward Performance Objectives

A number of instructional procedures have been designed to maximize the educational advantages of a course where the goals are explicit and organized in a logical sequence. The impetus for the technological development of the performance-oriented course came with the "invention" of the teaching machine and programmed learning by B. F. Skinner (1954). The teaching machine rather quickly ran its course since it turned out to be a relatively trivial page-turning device; the concept of programming has survived, but less as a technology than as a model for performance-oriented teaching in general. The original manuals on how to write a programmed text directed the teacher-author to construct a step-by-step sequence of "frames" to lead the student from his point of entry to the desired "terminal behaviors." Mager's *Preparing Objectives for Programmed Instruction* (1962) was probably the best known early statement and became the "bible" for reconstituting the curriculum.

In principle, this emphasis on performance objectives is consistent with the values of a pragmatic generation of students, but neither teachers nor students like to be fenced in by a tightly programmed presentation. Thus, the next phase in the development of performance-oriented instruction was to loosen up the programmed "frames" into larger and more meaningful units of study. The performance criterion is applied to a succession of "modular" units (a chapter, or units in a specially prepared syllabus), and the student demonstrates a satisfactory level of mastery before going on to the next unit. This basic arrangement can best be described as *self-paced supervised study*, although specific variations have been presented under such headings as: precision teaching, mastery learning, the Keller Plan, contingency contracting, contract teaching, modular instruction, and personalized systems of instruction (PSI). Specific references to these instructional technologies are given in Chapter 7, since the principle of reinforcement is one of the major components in the rationale of performance-oriented courses of study. The application or performance-oriented instruction is most easily made in training programs for specific skills and for factual knowledge. The development of these procedures has been most active in the science and engineering areas where the internal sequence of topics may lend itself to the preplanned hierarchical arrangement. In the social sciences and humanities, the same interest in goal-oriented study is expressed in the development of interdisciplinary courses geared to specified goals, issues, and problems. In this setting, discipline-based categories of knowledge are selectively retrieved as needed to promote the analysis of the problem-objectives making up the new course of inquiry.

At the Corner of Academy and Main

The curricular theme of the Free University gives emphasis to problem-oriented interdisciplinary instruction. In this environment the student has greater freedom to determine what he studies, without being hemmed in by department and college requirements and conventions. In his survey of "The Free School Movement," Allen Graubard (1972) identifies A. S. Neill's *Summerhill* as the prototype example of the assumption that ". . . children are naturally curious and motivated to learn by their own interests and desires. The most important condition for nurturing this natural interest is freedom supported by adults who enrich the environment and offer help. In contrast, coercion and regimentation only inhibit emotional and intellectual development" (p. 352). Among college students this urge for intellectual freedom is expressed in many different forms but one theme seems to persist: to organize one's inquiry in concert with others toward objectives of personal and/or social relevance. In most of the larger institutions various curricular arrangements, e.g., the Bulletin Board course, Course Mart, Outreach, and many of the living-learning and cluster-college offerings, allow faculty and students to get together for mutual analysis of *problems.* Credit courses, such as Environmental Economics, Peace, and Racism, have been around for some time. The new flavor is found in: Violence, Love, Alienation, Community, and the like. (Their counterparts in engineering, medicine, law, dentistry, veterinary science, and so forth would be on less existential dimensions!) The titles change with the mood of the times but not the basic structure. Students elect these offerings with enthusiasm and generally assume an attitude of being accountable for their own progress and achievement.

Students enroll in these courses not to avoid intellectual work but for the positive purpose of becoming involved with a systematic, interdisciplinary analysis of a complex problem that is personally relevant. Their reading, research, and discussions are focused toward issues often left out of a traditional department-based offering. Left to themselves, student-controlled courses tend to stress short-term, here-and-now problems in contrast to the longer perspectives that senior teachers like to emphasize.

The ways of teaching problem-oriented courses vary from independent study to lectures by a public figure, although the discussion group is the usual mode for conducting the class. In general these are less tightly structured courses in which examinations are the exception and pass-fail or credit-no entry grading is the rule. The textbook format does not apply since it can be assumed that if a suitable text were available the course itself would not have been created. Extensive reading lists are compiled by interested teachers and students, and field trips are popular. These courses vary as to where they meet and how often, who are the teachers and who are the students, and the sources of information, but they do not wander far from their common purpose of focusing the talent and the resources of the university more directly on the problems of the real world and the experiences of real people. "Alternative" education has now become institutionalized and presumably new alternatives will, in time, turn up. In the meantime, the "University without Walls" (1972) and other forms of "nontraditional" study (Samuel Gould and Patricia Cross, 1972; Ohmer Milton, 1972; Empire State College, 1972) are receiving a great deal of attention. These problem/performance-oriented courses of study are especially appropriate for the current expansion in adult education.

Guidelines for Course Planning

Without being hooked by either extreme of behaviorism or humanism, a subject-matter teacher can organize a course of study in terms of its three main components: the objectives, the instructional arrangements consistent with the demands to be placed on the students, and the methods for evaluating achievement of these objectives.

1. *The objectives.* The teacher first views the outside world (or the follow-up course) to assess the knowledge, skills, and attitudes to be required of his students. He is forming his instructional objectives. In prerequisite courses, the objectives are more or less taken care of by the sequential nature of the curriculum. In certain professional areas, the teacher

may be in conflict with his own best judgment as to course objectives and the kind of content information that he knows will be needed when taking an external examination, such as the National Boards in medicine.

Another conflict may be between the teacher and his students. In small classes it is not particularly difficult to negotiate the differences about objectives, but in large lecture courses the objectives are operationally defined by the procedures used in evaluation and grading. One objection to large classes is that the teacher makes most of the decisions as to what is learned and when.

In survey courses, seminars, interdisciplinary offerings, and in many other teaching settings, where some flexibility as to course content is permissible, an appropriate strategy for the teacher is to establish the *outer limits, the boundaries* within which the individual student or small interest groups of students can specify their own goals. The teacher must be realistic in deciding how much freedom he can allow, and must state the limits within which his subject-matter expertise is pertinent. The principle of a performance-oriented course is not compromised, and the advantage of participation is gained, when students mark out a subset of objectives with which they want to become involved. Initial responsibility, however, rests with the teacher with his knowledge of the content area of his course and the available resources.

2. *The instructional arrangements.* Having settled on the objectives (or the strategies for their modification), the next step involves the different skills and abilities required to master the subject matter. To what extent, for example, is memorizing required, or rapid reading, concept attainment, interpersonal

sensitivities, analysis of value judgments, and so forth? This assessment will lead to decisions about the instructional arrangements which will most likely support the exercise of these skills and abilities. Students differ in these respects and since formal course prerequisites are unreliable indicators of what a student knows and what he can do, diagnostic information should be obtained at the beginning of the course.

3. *Evaluation.* This third step requires that the objectives of a course be consistent with the way it is taught. A well-organized course will almost teach itself and evaluation follows naturally and is continuous. No single blueprint will apply and a good teacher demonstrates his talent by establishing an instructional plan whereby each student receives evaluative information when needed to direct his course of study toward the agreed upon objectives. The goading, threatening, punishing function of the teacher is replaced by positive and constructive feedback in the progress of achieving goals that have meaning and value to the student. The summative grade at the end of a course is relatively unimportant. It says too little and comes too late.

The integration of objectives, teaching, and evaluation takes many forms. It is easier in some subject areas than in others and is more congenial to the habits and values of some teachers than of others. But nearly all will agree that the value of what is to be learned lies beyond the classroom door. The carryover in information and skill from one site to another is a long-standing issue in learning theory—the transfer of learning.

Chapter 4

The Transfer of Learning

Good instruction leads a student to know more than he has learned; to acquire knowledge, skills, and attitudes that can be carried over for use at other times and in different settings. This carryover is called *transfer of learning* and comes close to being the essence of the educational ideal. In reality the management of instruction and the goals of learning are dominated by here-and-now pressures of final examinations and degree requirements. Understandably, some degree of satisfaction is felt by the teacher for a job well done when he looks over the results of the final examination and sees the impressive amount of information students have gained from his course. College students are indeed good learners; many are born and bred to achieve "high marks" but this is not the proper goal of instruction. The best measure of good teaching is the performance of students after they leave the classroom—one year or ten years later, or, hopefully, for a lifetime. Research and theory have addressed the conceptual problem of transfer of learning and offer a solid base for instructional planning.

The Transfer Model

For convenience of analysis, learning theorists distinguish between *original learning* (when information is first acquired) and *retention* and *transfer.* The conditions that prevail at the time of original learning and during the retention interval have an important influence on the transfer of learning effects. Material that is learned by rote memorizing will not show up in the transfer setting as well as does material that is more meaningful. More than eighty-five years ago Herman Ebbinghaus demonstrated the distressingly steep forgetting-curve for memorized verbal material. Subsequent studies have confirmed that most memorized information is soon forgotten and that forgetting starts immediately—as soon as the learning or the reviewing and cramming stops. Figure 1 is a schematic sketch of the retention characteristics of two types of learning: rote and meaningful. The contrast in retention effects shows clearly why meaningfulness is such a critical factor in the transfer of learning.

The projection of the retention curve for meaningful material along the time line is branched in the diagram to show the "usual" and the "ideal" levels of performance. In either case, the teacher should forego impressive coverage of factual and taxonomic material and direct his students toward the principles, procedures, and general rules that will help students recognize the meaning of specific, factual, and concrete events later in the transfer setting. This is a fundamental point because meaningfulness is the most effective single countervailing influence to the steep forgetting curve. Rather than being forgotten, meaningful material continues to become better organized as the student finds ways to apply and to

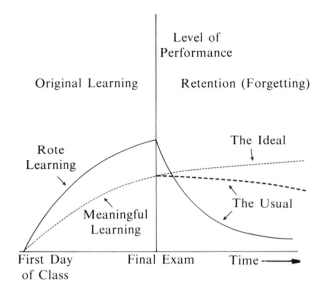

Fig. 1. Retention of rote and meaningful learning

utilize it in situations outside the classroom. The gradual increment of meaningful material, rather than its gradual decline, is almost entirely a function of the depth and breadth of meaning of these "ideas" for the individual student. This determines how readily they are retrieved for application in a variety of settings such as reading, television viewing, and personal and professional problem solving.

This potential transfer effect is not a learning theory trick; it is a common phenomenon of everyday life, namely, "The longer I live the more convinced I am that X (concept, principle, generalization) is true." A particular insight or idea or observation gains in meaning and utility as a function of subsequent experiences and as it becomes integrated with material the student has already learned. The practical experience of raising children, for example, verifies the *meaning* of the textbook concepts parents once learned in a psychology course even though they have probably forgotten who did what experiments and under what conditions.

The steady rise of the "ideal" retention curve in Figure 1 and its transfer of learning benefits are the result of three conditions that prevail at the time of original classroom learning:

1. The substantive information is relevant to the anticipated transfer situations; it has *intrinsic carry-over value*. Neither the teacher nor the student knows in detail what these future applications might be but the subject-matter teacher is the better judge of the potential transfer benefits of the substantive units in his course.

2. The teacher defines his course objectives in terms of a *limited number of larger "ideas"* (principles, generalizations, procedures, attitudes, and values) rather than in terms of a mass of factual information.

3. Information is *thoroughly learned* and routine procedures of teaching and testing are changed if need be. Each student should have the opportunity to "package" the course content in his own language so that, over a period of time, he will more readily recognize confirming and nonconfirming recurrences of the generalized principles learned in the classroom. (See Chapter 9.)

Theories of Transfer Learning

Few will question the importance of transfer, but many will question any particular approach for bringing it about. The roots of theories about transfer reach to the very sources of Western culture. Greek education initially emphasized the development of the body. The gymnastic program was later supplemented with the study of music, which was thought to promote harmony of spirit, and oratory, which was believed to develop the quick and logical mind. This conception of education prevailed for many centuries.

Transfer via Mental Discipline

Medieval monasticism directed the complete development of the soul (self) by means of rigorous schedules of study, meditation, hard work, and self-abnegation, and this point of view carried over into the medieval university from which the modern university takes its shape. The curriculum was largely dominated by the teaching of Latin, Greek, theology, and history as necessary tools for the priestly function. In the seventeenth century, higher education began to expand its functions and the professors of these first-line disciplines required all students, regardless of their professional or personal goals, to enroll in their "core" courses. The doctrine of mental discipline emerged as their relatively uncomplicated theory of education.

This theory held that the educational value of a subject lay especially in the mental effort required to master it. In 1706, John Locke used the term "transfer" in his *Conduct of the Understanding* in which he expressed the discipline position:

> Would you have a man reason well, you must use him to it betimes, exercise his mind in observing the connection of ideas and following them in train. Nothing does this better than mathematics, which therefore I think should be taught to all those who have the time and the opportunity, not so much to make them mathematicians as to make them reasonable creatures. . . . that having got the way of reasoning, which that study necessarily brings the mind to, they might be able to

transfer it to other parts of knowledge as they shall have the occasion. (Fowler, 1890)

It followed in the minds of some that the benefits of education were those derived from the coercion and discipline required to survive a standardized curriculum and a rigid sequence of examinations. Generations of students since have spent demanding hours in classroom and homework assignments designed to steel mind and character for the coming tests of strength after graduation. Many teachers dedicated to preparing the student to become the "liberally educated man" believe that rigorous study of a given subject will, in fact, improve the student's mind and strengthen his mental muscles to better master other subjects and to improve his intellectual analysis of world events for the rest of his life. Their point is well taken but not their theory.

Transfer via Content

Formal research on transfer theory began as a search for an explanation to counter the discipline theory. At the turn of this century, Edward Thorndike and Robert Woodworth, colleagues at Columbia University, were trying to understand how student performance in one course—English—might be influenced by the prior learning of other material—Latin. Their main interpretive emphasis was on the concept of *identical elements* which postulated that the transfer from "A" to "B" was made via the information common to the two situations. In the interest of achieving tighter experimental controls, the laboratory studies in the 1930s and 1940s were narrowed down to relatively simple units of behavior—how the left hand profits from what the right hand learns.

A number of investigators felt that the molecular

fixation on the stimulus-response aspects of transfer was inadequate for purposes of theoretical development or for educational application. Research attention was thus directed to the *nonspecific factors* such as improving a person's ability to learn how to learn (see Chapter 8). One interesting series of studies (Harry Harlow, 1949) started from the uncomplicated observation that both animals and humans profit from practice; they learn from experience. In a typical experiment monkeys were faced with a simple discrimination task: learning that the raisin is always under the blue box, never under the red, regardless of position. Having mastered this information, they were presented with a different task: to learn that the raisin is always under the smaller of the two stimulus objects. Each discrimination task was completely mastered before moving to further problems such as discriminating shapes or spatial position. Harlow found that his subjects gradually increased the rate at which they mastered these successive tasks; they were learning how to learn and had acquired a "learning set" which speeded up the transfer from one task to the next.

Transfer by *generalization* was another conception (Judd, 1908) presented as a replacement for the discipline theory. Subsequent research has examined specific questions of how generalizations are formed and what exactly are the transferable elements. One answer is given by the *transposition* studies initiated by the Gestalt (cognitive theory) school of psychology. Animal subjects were trained to discriminate between two stimulus patterns that differ, for example, as to size or as to brightness (see Fig. 2). It was found that the animals were able to transpose the "larger than" or the "brighter than" principle to the test (transfer) situation even though the former negative

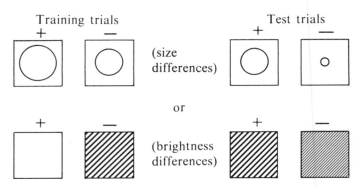

Fig. 2. Transposition training and testing

stimulus was now positive. Human learners are, of course, much more adept at sifting out specific relationships which may later be transposed for effective problem-solving application.

Research and theory today cast the classical transfer of learning problem into more specific categories such as concept utilization, problem solving, and the role of language transformations. This latter is especially important since a college student lives and learns in a world of words. He learns how to learn with words; he uses words to stimulate and respond, to represent his cognitive maps and abstract ideas, to test his generalizations, to represent his motives, and to assess the relevance of what he has learned. Linguistic analysis has been particularly active on the research and theory side—mediated associations, semantic differential, linguistic transformations, verbal encoding, verbal conditioning—but applications of this analysis to educational tasks have not been extensive.

Once the student leaves the classroom he is gone, and follow-up information about his success elsewhere is, at best, sporadic. Understandably, then, the teacher tends to emphasize original learning more than how well material is retained or carried over to other places. This emphasis is not misplaced since research confirms that good original learning is a necessary although not a sufficient condition for retention and transfer. A further research refinement is also consistent with the observation of experienced teachers—the importance of having learned to manage the methodology and the problem-solving procedures within a given field. The *processes* involved in generating and using knowledge make up, therefore, an especially important component of the "substantive content" of a course of study. Nearly every department wrestles with the problem of how to teach its own set of scholarly procedures and scientific methodologies. Capabilities of this order almost automatically carry over to the transfer settings if these process skills were taught in a way that stressed their general application beyond the site of original learning.

Training for Professional Practice

Education for professional service demonstrates the transfer paradigm, since the relationship between original learning and its application in the field is specifically planned for. The return of information to the classroom from the field should influence the objectives of the training program: to relate the educational program more directly to the career requirements of professional practice.

On the basis of a systematic survey of professional practice, William Brown (1967) found that practicing dentists did not fully utilize the dental assistant as a resource for extending dental service to the community. Simply knowing about "four-handed dentistry" from reading, lectures, and demonstrations did not carry over into practice. The instructional program was therefore modified to give each clinical student considerable practice toward acquiring the habit of working with the dental assistant *before* entering into his professional career.

Legal education is seeking various means to revise its curricular goals in the light of contemporary social conditions and their demands on the profession (Carrington, 1971). More concretely, the Council on Legal Education for Professional Responsibility, Inc. (CLEPR) has supported the development of clinical instruction and "discussions of clinical education now center around how best to conduct a clinical program rather than whether or not there should be a clinical program at all." (Rubino, 1972, p. ii). Law school teachers treasure their diversity, and no single curricular or instructional plan can satisfy the many-faceted dimensions of legal education. Teachers know full well that neither they nor their students can anticipate all the specific problems and information resources that will later be needed by the practicing attorney. Inevitably, therefore, instructional objectives are defined in terms of the structure, dimensions, and boundaries of concept, principles, rules, moral standards, and generalizations that apply to the broad practice of law. The reshaping and applying of these principles has generally been left to on-the-job training of the apprentice lawyer. The goal of CLEPR is to reduce this gap between theory and practice.

Medical schools seem always to be engaged in educational experiments aimed at improving a student's preparation for his work in the clinic and the hospital, and for practice in the field. The one-time breach between the first two years of basic science instruction and the second two years of clinical training is being bridged through student contact with patients in the first year and continuing through the successive years of medical school training. In the language of this chapter, this kind of experience is intended to improve the transfer of textbook knowledge for understanding and treatment of individual patients.

Professionals training in social work, education, clinical psychology, and nursing and others have wrestled with in-the-field training problems for a long time and have learned that supervised direction is usually helpful in carrying over the abstractions of the classroom to the concrete reality of professional services for individual persons. Ideally, therefore, these "clinical" experiences should be extension and application of "textbook" knowledge rather than being parallel or otherwise quite separate from the content emphasis given on campus. Over and over again, graduates of professional schools express the opinion that their in-the-field experiences were among the most valuable components in their education.

The Transfer of Learning and Liberal Arts Education

Liberal arts education is presumed to be useful to the student wherever he goes and in whatever perspective he views himself, his community, and civilization in general. This is a heavy assignment and especially when in competition with the specific appeals of vocational/professional training. It is not sufficient to defend a program of study in which the objectives are undefined and in which the means of instruction are too often self-serving to the faculty. The transfer idea is implicit in, indeed central to, liberal education and teachers are responsible for identifying content material important for the long term and for helping students to organize this information in such

a way as to put order into their views of the world
and of themselves.

Science Instruction in the Liberal Arts

Internal relevance—the transfer of information from
one course to another within a given discipline
area—is the oldest and most frequently used argument for either defending or changing a department-
based curriculum. For many years the introductory
science courses have been taught as if all students
would go on to be chemists, physicists, or biologists.
As Professor Richard Crane (1968) points out, students ". . . are not going to continue forever to sub-
mit to the physics requirement unless they can be
shown reasons that it is essential to their career objectives." The science disciplines have been self-
critical in analyzing the changing nature (toward
transfer value) of their educational task. And these
redirections are being made without compromising
the integrity of the discipline. Good physics *is* being
taught to make better poets (March, 1970).

Physics has been hit hard by the imbalance of
supply and demand for teachers, but there were
"deeper worries" as the Commission on College
Physics (1971) examined the educational plight of its
prestigious discipline. The data in Table 1 reflects
aggressive action by many physics departments to
improve the educational relevance of their subject
area; to extend the transfer-of-learning objectives.
These changes are not unique to physics; similar revisions are reported by most of the science disciplines.

The Social Sciences

Not only are students asking questions about the university's response to social problems, they are also

seeking depth and breadth of knowledge for their own better understanding of society and its tangle of problems. Teachers in the social sciences face a challenging task in relating course content to the transfer objectives inherent in these concerns of their students.

TABLE 1
INNOVATIONS IN CONTENT OF UNDERGRADUATE OFFERINGS
IN PHYSICS

Category	Percentage of 250 Schools Reporting
Environmental problems	36.4
Urban problems	6.8
Weapons	7.2
History of science	20.4
Transportation	9.6
Interaction of science with society	34.4
Energy and power	24.0
Philosophy of science	27.2

SOURCE: Adapted from Ronald Blum, 1971.

In his national survey of undergraduate instruction in psychology, James Kulik (1973) described departmental adaptations to societal problem solving. Courses in applied psychology, for example, seem *not* to be the answer and this cookbook offering is given less frequently than in former years. The curricular task is to maintain a healthy balance between short- and long-term applications of social-science offerings. At Boston College, for example, a strong social-problems curriculum initiated in 1967 was modified three years later toward more conventional goals. Kulik reports that undergraduate students are a constructive influence in resolving conflicts related to the transfer of learning needs of the nonmajors, the goals of the aspiring Ph.D.s, the subject-matter interests of the faculty, and the awareness of many teachers and students of their responsibility to carry out "research *in* and *with* the community" as a means for bringing about social change.

As the teacher for a final-term course for undergraduate majors in psychology, the author conducted a twelve-year "experiment" on how best to help students reorganize what they had learned from lecture, text, and reference reading to give this information more meaning in the off-campus world (Ericksen, 1955). The first assignment asked students to look ahead and to examine the critical events and personal roles for which they were preparing. Each student described ten such transfer-of-learning objectives— being a good parent, earning a living, accepting frustration and defeat, being an enlightened citizen, and so forth. The second assignment called for a descriptive paragraph about each of ten "concepts, laws, or principles which you believe to be most significant for application to most of the transfer situations derived from the first assignment." At the following class session a process of sorting, sifting, and combining produced a list of fifteen to eighteen "great ideas" in psychology. The subject-matter objectives for the course were thus established as these concepts became the topical theme for essays on their transfer applications.

The students worked hard. The nature of each assignment precluded extensive paraphrasing of familiar texts or library references. Each student wrote his own "relevance" manual designed around transferable ideas as chapter headings. These seniors had spent four years assimilating information against a criterion of achievement examinations. In this course no examinations were given. Each set of weekly papers was evaluated by the teacher in terms of how well the student could extend psychological principles into the realities of daily living. The favorable reactions from students during the course (and later as alumni) were confirmation that this type of class procedure did promote the transfer value of their liberal arts education in psychology.

The Humanities

When a liberal arts student registers to study logic and language, Shakespeare, a classical or modern language, the history of Western civilization, or contemporary literature, he is presumed to be preparing himself to make enlightened decisions at various choice points for the rest of his life: what television channels to watch, what to select from paperback book racks, where to travel, which voting levers to pull, petitions to sign, museums to visit, and meetings to attend. The transfer paradigm does indeed apply to the humanities, that is, to the specific courses of study. Considering the educational complexity of this core curricular area, one must guard against easy generalizations about what instruction in the humanities does or does not do. Even within the boundaries of a particular course, a student cannot assess its potential transfer advantages without knowing the specific objectives, and these are rarely static and fixed. Freshman English, for example, is almost a universal offering in higher education. Introduced at Harvard University about one hundred years ago as a combination of grammar, rhetoric, composition, and literature, it spread across the land under a variety of labels (Leonard Greenbaum, 1970). At one time or at one place the emphasis might be on: the mechanics of composition, the study of literature in general, a specific instructional theme such as Shakespeare, or more recently as a freshman seminar serving as an orienting discussion group for the beginning student. It has survived by adapting to the changing educational requirements of successive generations of students or by meeting the special needs of students in different kinds of institutions.

In another field of the humanities, Professor Gerald F. Else (1972) justifies the educational (transfer) value of the classics directly and explicitly in terms of its contribution to the understanding of complex human affairs. He points out that in the beginning language was studied as a tool:

> The notion that an educated man has to have mastered at least one foreign language began with the Romans. They studied Greek to gain access to the ideas of the Greek philosophers, scientists, historians, statesmen, dramatists, poets. . . . [Gradually the] means came to be regarded as the ends; the substantive content of classical studies began to be limited to grammar. Students slogged through Gaul with Caesar, but too often no one let them in on what Caesar was up to. (p. 6)

Professor Else makes it quite clear that the effective teacher of the classics must know philosophy and history and be able to recognize the strengths and the limits of historical analogy. Comparing the fate of Athens with America, for example, is judged to be an important means "of working our way toward a better understanding of our situation. . . . we Americans suffer from cultural and historical myopia, and much of the responsibility for that must rest with the scholars and teachers in our colleges and universities" (p. 15). The meaning of the message given by the language being learned must not be set aside by a fixation on the mechanics of the language itself.

Studies in the humanities are as important as they have ever been but the emphasis now swings toward the direct worth of what is learned for adding understanding to the student's perception of the human scene. As he shapes his own life style, a student is influenced by his analysis of man and society, by his personal identification with strong characters from literature, history, and philosophy and the ideas they evidence as having enduring worth. Perhaps in the humanities more than in other areas, the selective filter is provided by the individual student.

Practical Considerations

This chapter has emphasized that the transfer benefits from a course of study derive from the *meaning* of what is learned rather than as a *side effect* from memorizing or other variations of tedious mental effort. Direction from the teacher with respect to the following five points, will facilitate the instructional conditions for the transfer of learning:

1. The teacher's first contribution is to identify and label those principles, attitudes, skills, and problem-solving procedures that, in his judgment, have a predicted *half-life*, for example, of at least ten years. Students do, in fact, have a legitimate complaint if their assignments are directed primarily to the acquisition of information that is quickly outdated or that is limited in its scope of application. Situation-specific information usually has less transfer value than do the more abstract generalizations on which students can draw in the face of new experiences. Chapter 3 was an elaboration of this first step.

2. If a test is coming up the next day, a student will study and remember material differently than if his *intention* is to prepare for an examination a month away or for application in an interdisciplinary

setting two years hence. Students are realistic and their own "set" to remember is influenced by the kind of information expected on tests and quizzes and *also* by their own perceptions of the long-range value of this material. Students should find, therefore, that the examinations they take (and other evaluating criteria) measure the quality of original learning *and* their ability to project this information into the transfer setting.

3. *Overlearning* (going beyond the minimum requirements to recognize, recall, or utilize what is being learned) aids transfer. Overlearning is especially helpful if it gives a student the opportunity to review what he is learning under conditions that approximate the transfer setting; to "practice under game conditions." The important increment resulting from overlearning is the student's clearer perception of the boundaries of a topic and the meaning of its intrinsic structure. Drill, memorizing, and mechanical rehearsal are inefficient forms of overlearning effort.

4. A teaching emphasis on transfer effects, per se, will not compensate for poor original learning. Long before learning theory became formalized, teachers recognized that *understanding* is the first measure of whether a given body of knowledge has been mastered. If a student does not know the meaning of what he has learned in the first place, it is unlikely that he will retrieve and use the information at some future date. Cramming for a test may enable a student to pass it, but organizing and reorganizing information for purposes of understanding is a far more productive means of study.

5. Knowledge is power, and education is an active agent for change but well-meaning people often differ as to what changes should be made or brought about. Discussions of the application of knowledge to

particular issues or situations, therefore, nearly always involve *value judgments* by both teachers and students. The ability to explore these values with humility and yet with genuine concern is a significant component of good teaching and one which is especially important in promoting the transfer process. The best strategy of the teacher is to help students see the high transfer *value* of what they are learning here and now.

Chapter 5

Self-Esteem

No single chapter can cover the subject of motivation since the boundaries of this topic meander in undefined directions and reflect nearly all aspects of a student's past and current engagements. The present treatment aims at one theme important for the teacher: the pervasive nature of self-related motivation in the lives of students. The following two chapters (Chapter 6, The Attitides and Values Students Study By, and Chapter 7, The Theory and Practice of Reinforcement) detail the management of motivation and its relation to learning. Chapter 10, Person to Person Interaction in the Classroom, also analyzes the dynamics of the instructional setting. Obviously, motivation and learning are intertwined, but understanding particular expressions of this relation is complicated by the fact that while the end-products of learning can be seen, motivation is an inferential concept. To explain the *why* of behavior or to account for the "causes" that direct and propel the way people talk, write, work (or do not work) always involves some degree of speculation.

Self-esteem represents a base-line motive yet antidates the outpouring of theories, doctrines, polemics, and mottos about: self-identity, self-realization, self-fulfillment, self-actualization, ego-involvement, and the like. The discourse among students along these lines expresses their desire, if not their demand, to be recognized and accepted as autonomous individuals rather than as anonymous members of the "student body." Students differ one from the other in the depth of their concern with self-related matters and the means for expression but the motive to maintain and to enhance one's concept of oneself touches, to some extent, nearly everything a student does. Socrates advised to "know thyself" and students are taking him at his word.

Socrates also said, "When the soul and body are united, then nature orders the soul to rule and govern, and the body to obey and serve." To "know thyself," therefore, was a thoroughly cognitive inquiry, and Greek sophistry was controlled intellectual manipulation. A college faculty also distrusts anti-intellectual modes of persuasion and thinks of itself as a body of rational men, and they like to project this image to their students. True, students are curious and they want to learn, but as young adults many of their interests are self-related and often with only cursory attention to discipline-based knowledge.

Robert Blackburn (1968) diagnosed mounds of interview reports to offer a refreshing close-up of seven days in the lives of twenty-one freshmen at the University of Michigan. These interviews revealed the personal dynamics of typical first-year students; the expectations they bring into the classroom and the values against which they weigh what they are asked to learn:

> The most striking aspect of these interviews is the extent to which they reveal how profoundly students are

concerned with themselves, with their own personal and social development. . . . . Each appears to have set his own private expectations for a given course and to have measured success or failure against this yardstick rather than against an absolute standard. . . .

Concern for self pervades their 'non-academic' lives as well. The students' curiosity about themselves is almost hypnotic and occasionally directs them into situations they know will be frustrating and distressful and will leave them depressed.

The conflict between Doing and Being is a clean contrast but the first mistake for the teacher would be to oversimplify motivational explanations for all the interesting and unexpected things that students do. The motivation to survive in college is partly a push from home and the past and partly a pull toward the new aspirations and personal goals that are beginning to shape up. These motives are the raw material for educational direction as influenced by the faculty, the curriculum, the social impact of peers, and the climate that characterizes the institution as a whole.

Based on his experiences as a teacher and as a researcher-in-depth on the personal development of college students, Professor Donald R. Brown (1968) summarized the three main points of educational interchange between the school and the individual student:

1. Freeing of impulse through the opportunity to learn and to deal with human experience in imagination through contact with literature, philosophy, and the arts while not directly committing oneself. The value of empathy through imagination in education should not be underestimated.

2. Enlightenment of conscience to the point

where the individual believes in what he does because he has arrived at a moral code by reasoned
judgment. Diversity, training in disciplines, analysis
of thought, and a tolerant but committed faculty
whose values are made explicit to the student are in-
valuable.

3. The development of finer perceptions and integration of personal beliefs so that the student, as he
increases his scope, becomes more discriminating in
the control of his own behavior.

The paradox is that education often fosters the kind of
growth that produces stress more rapidly than it develops the student's ability to handle stress. This may
be inevitable. (p.5)

Unrest and stress on campus is normal, natural,
and possibly a necessary condition if the classroom
and the college are to have appreciable impact on
students. Insofar as docility means apathy and boredom, not much is likely to happen toward expanding
the concept of self by these students. An exciting educational climate is one in which students sense that
they have a lot to learn and that they must also press
for significant changes in their own beliefs.

Conceptual Models of Motivation

Speculation about the mainsprings of human action is
as old as literature, philosophy, and folklore. Interest
continues as personality theory today screens and
combines these older ideas with the new research
findings and views about the motivating qualities of
human experience. Nevertheless, no analysis of the
dynamics of human behavior would be complete
without initial reference to psychoanalysis. Sigmund
Freud (and Alfred Adler and Carl Jung) made the
first major contributions toward correcting the motivational oversight that had, for so long, prevailed in

the philosophical, religious, and social views of human nature.

Psychoanalysis

Freud's particular conceptions about human dynamics may now be questioned, but the essence of his argument seems timeless: motivation controls behavior; man is not the rational master of his own actions. In Freud's view, individual behavior derived from interactions among the Id, the Ego, and the Superego. Adler placed his emphasis on the individual's striving for superiority, the need for power and to reduce feelings of inferiority. Jung stressed the primary need for self-actualization as the guiding factor in personality development.

In any case, society objected and its massive resistance is reminder of the cultural buffers that are raised to guard against unconventional notions about the "inner man." To be knocked off the rational-man pedestal was bad enough but to have Sex Power replace Will Power was almost more than post-Victorian society could accept. The tumult has subsided and the discussion of human dynamics is now more penetrating and revealing as a consequence of our enriched understanding of the self. The concepts derived from psychoanalysis as a systematic theory are not, however, directly pertinent to the educational setting. In practice, psychoanalysis deals with sickness, instruction deals with health; the classroom is not a clinic and the teacher is not a therapist.

Contemporary approaches to the dynamics of student behavior will more likely serve the interests of the teacher, especially the conceptual models stemming from research and theory on learning, personality development, and social behavior. Psychoanalysis, for instance, is essentially noncognitive in orientation in contrast to the approach described in the following section which emphasizes how the learner *perceives* the relations between himself and his environment. Of particular interests are those points of view derived from observing the activities of students as subjects in the research setting and also in their normal affairs in class and on campus.

The Motivation to Learn

For almost a quarter century J. W. Atkinson (1964, 1966, 1970) has directed a research program on human motivation, and his central finding is especially relevant to education: student performance is a joint function of relatively stable personality characteristics *interacting* with the variable properties of the immediate environment. The key word is "interacting" since the personality-motivational characteristics of a student function as a selective screen through which he perceives the teacher and the class. The *anxious* student, for example, will respond to the "challenging" style of a teacher and to the competition from his classmates quite differently than will a student whose perceptions of a teacher and a class are directed by a strong need to *achieve*. This interaction principle has been confirmed with other personality characteristics. In classes in which the instructor was judged to be warm and friendly, students high in *affiliation* motive (to be liked, to be accepted in a group) received relatively higher grades than they received in classes in which they did not perceive the instructor as friendly. Similarly, students high in *power* motive received relatively higher grades in classes in which they were encouraged to volunteer ideas.

Most of the research and theory building by Atkinson and his students has been oriented toward the need to achieve and its corollary, the need to avoid failure. The *achievement* motive—a strong desire to compete successfully against a standard of excellence—and the motive to avoid *failure*—a strong predisposition to experience shame or humiliation when one fails—have both been studied in some detail in the school setting (O'Connor, 1964). Students differ from one another in the strength of these two motives, and these differences have a consistent effect on behavior in competitive situations. For example, experimental subjects (students) who had been classified as being highly motivated toward achievement solve more problems, persist longer in the face of failure, and set more realistic goals for themselves than subjects low in achievement motive. Those subjects who could best be described as wanting to avoid failure solve fewer problems, persist less after failure, and set less realistic goals than subjects who are low in this motive. Measures of achievement-related motives predict performance only when the situation is structured so that it is clear that performance will be evaluated against some standard of excellence. In a relaxed situation, differences in these motives are not associated with performance. In brief, a situation where achievement will be graded competitively will generally enhance the performance of students for whom achievement motive is relatively strong and will produce performance decrements in those for whom motive to avoid failure is relatively strong.

Many college teachers are, themselves, good examples of the upwardly mobile, high-achieving norm of middle class society. Students with similar dynamics are quickly spotted and generally supported in their efforts toward conventional goals of high academic achievement. A student low in the need for achievement is not necessarily poorly motivated to learn; his interests may lie elsewhere or his performance may be directed by other motives such as anxiety or by the need for affiliation.

Thus, classroom conditions favorable for some students may be unfavorable for others. A perceptive teacher will make appropriate adjustments in the light of these motivational differences just as he would for differences in verbal ability and academic background. Adjustments in testing and grading procedures, for example, may help anxious students meet the prevailing competition in the classroom through more frequent testing, take-home exams, report writing options, and the like. A tutor can rather easily adapt to the motivational characteristics of each student but the teacher of a large class faces a demanding test of skill in recognizing and using such differences. If it were possible to arrange such a "matching," it might be expected that learning would be better under teachers whose natural pattern of involvement and interaction with people was compatible with the incentives of his students. Sectioning of large classes on the basis of the motivational characteristics of students and the classroom style of the teacher is not generally feasible but it might be considered in individual instances.

Curiosity and Intrinsic Motivation

Lower animals as well as humans have an intrinsic need to explore and to experience change. As D. E. Berlyne (1960) has pointed out, we can accomodate to excitement or to boredom for just so long before seeking outlets for the need for change. Not every topic in a course will trigger the interests of every student, and for reasons that are both biological and experiential in nature, every student should have some freedom to follow the lead of his own curiosity; to satisfy the need to explore something that may be of interest only to himself.

This intrinsic need to learn and to achieve, to cope with and master the environment is called "competence motivation" by Robert White (1955) who developed his conception out of his teaching, observing, and research interviewing of students at Harvard. The satisfaction of this motive is realized during the process of achieving mastery and resolving one's intellectual curiosity. Self esteem is enhanced by demonstrating to oneself the ability to interact with and to cope with a personal, social, or educational problem. The enthusiasm shown by students who seek the opportunity for independent study illustrates the driving power of intellectual curiosity; the intensity and the effectiveness of students when they become "involved." White's conception and Berlyne's extensive research on curiosity lend credence and support to the efforts of many teachers and schools to loosen up the patterns of instruction toward greater intellectual and personal freedom.

Despite the leveling effects of mass education, students continue to explore new ideas and to hold on to their personal interests. The acquisition of knowledge can be its own reward and the holding power of self-directed achievement is not limited to the superior student. A group of young adults in a correctional institution (McKee, 1964, 1973) studied a well-programmed unit on basic electronics. For probably the first time in their lives they enjoyed an intrinsically rewarding classroom experience and the formal application of this principle has been expanded. In a similar setting (Fader and Schaevitz, 1966), boys were encouraged to read or write about whatever they wished and were rewarded for what they accomplished rather than punished for what they had not read or said correctly. These near-illiterate adolescents learned to read and write, and one of them published a book of poetry.

Many of the conventions that shape the academic enterprise today are carried over from an earlier era when obedience was expected and conformity prevailed. Few of the students or faculty ventured to question what was to be learned and how it was to be taught. The motivational climate of docile acquiesence to authority, of coercion, punishment and threats of punishment would be too restrictive and "dehumanizing" for the values and academic interests of students now on campus.

With respect to motivation, the contrast between the old and the new is essentially the difference between *extrinsic* and *intrinsic* reward. The epitome of extrinsic motivational control is found in a typical laboratory-based study on human learning. Prearranged lists of words or a prose passage are memorized under the prescribed experimental conditions—the substance of what is being learned is a matter of almost complete indifference to the students. They are learning and earning by the hour and the paycheck is the reward. In contrast, the intrinsic satisfaction of discovery, understanding, and achieving personal meaning provides the principal motivation to learn in a well-taught course of study.

Self-Actualizing Motives

The late Abraham Maslow was a leading spokesman for existential-humanistic education. He was very much the academician but hardly of the "old school" although he recognized that studious preparation indepth was prerequisite to a student's personal development and the ultimate satisfaction of his self-actualizing needs. He rejected the extremism "of a mutually exclusive, antagonistic, either-or dichotomizing of instrinsic and extrinsic learning. Learning is not the enemy of personal growth (Maslow, 1970, p. 9). Maslow would argue, however, that it would be difficult if not impossible for a teacher to set forth learning objectives that would at the same time free the student to search, to inquire, to invent, to create, and to pursue the intrinsic values of knowing and understanding. Maslow presented humanism as the "Third Force" in education and his writings are widely referenced in support of the "open" schools.

Human needs start with the biological/physiological drives and carry through a hierarchy of social needs to the top level—the need for self-actualization, to be devoted to a task or objective outside oneself:

> Self-actualizing people are, without one single exception, involved in a cause outside their own skin, in something outside themselves. They are devoted, working at something, something that is very precious to them—some calling or vocation in the old sense, the priestly sense. They are working at something which fate has called them to somehow and which they work at and which they love, so that the work-joy dichotomy in them disappears. (Maslow, 1971, p. 43)

This merger of work and play is the ultimate expression of the value of intrinsic satisfactions.

Carl Rogers holds similar views and has also been a powerful influence in humanistic psychology and its place in education. The traditional school has stressed "cognitive learning"—the fixed body of stored knowledge—which is often unpleasant and difficult to learn and is poorly retained. To achieve what must be learned, the teacher is a "facilitator," promoting an environment which places his students in contact with life problems (or their simulation) as a form of "experiential" learning. Rogers feels that conventional schooling is based on assumptions that have the effect of curtailing the students "freedom to learn" (Rogers, 1969) in response to the intrinsic curiosity, the interests and needs that are distinctive for each student. These two sets of assumptions can be listed in contrast:

Assumptions Implicit in Current Education	*Assumptions Relevant to Significant Experiential Learning*
1. The student cannot be trusted to pursue his own learning.	1. Human beings have a natural potential for learning.
2. Presentation equals learning.	2. Significant learning takes place when the subject matter is perceived by the student as having relevance for his own purposes.
3. The aim of education is to accumulate brick upon brick of factual knowledge.	3. Much significant learning is acquired through doing.
4. The truth is known.	4. Learning is facilitated when the student participates responsibly in the learning process.
5. Constructive and creative citizens develop from passive learners.	5. Self-initiated learning, involving the whole person of the learner—feelings as well as intellect—is the most pervasive and lasting.

Assumptions Implicit in Current Education (Cont.)	*Assumptions Relevant to Significant Experiential Learning* (Cont.)
6. Evaluation is education; and education is evaluation.	6. Creativity in learning is best facilitated when self-criticism and self-evaluation are primary, and evaluation by others is of secondary importance.
	7. The most socially useful learning in the modern world is the learning of the process of learning, a continuing openness to experience, an incorporation into oneself of the process of change.
	(Adapted from Rogers, 1967, pp. 40–43)

Contemporary conceptual models of motivation were, for the most part, developed by men and women close to students and experienced as teachers but their theories were aimed at broader goals than the improvement of college teaching. They were structuring very basic views as to the nature of human nature. This pervasive nature of a theory of motivation tends to give it the quality of a philosophy of life, of education—as seen, for example, in the attitudes of the humanists and the behaviorists. A teacher's position with respect to motivation "theory" will be reflected in the climate of his classroom: if he or she is sensitive to the self-actualizing needs of students, a quite different teaching role will be seen than if the major concern is the need for high academic achievement.

This difference in "philosophy" of education tends to become exaggerated as an either/or disjunction. In the normal process of working with many students in one course after another, the teacher becomes involved with many motivation-related problems that test his understanding of student dynamics. The findings from the more general area of research on motivation offer helpful information toward this understanding and as guides for action when facing a motivational impasse.

Attributes of Motivation

Research has had quite a bit to say about *acquired drives,* that is, how different motives, interests, and ambitions are acquired (learned) through experience. "Negative" motives such as fear and anxiety are quickly learned. It is easy to teach fear, and far too many college students acquire high and persistent motivational states of anxiety about their courses. Teachers of mathematics and statistics often find, for example, that the best remedial help for the "slow" learner is to relieve the stress and anxiety that block understanding. Habits in general tend to be self-maintaining, and acquired motives are no exception to this behavioral rule. An acquired motivational pattern becomes a controlling factor in what the student will learn or will avoid. One student, for example, may have acquired a strong need to be a leader, another needs close affiliation with well-defined groups and both will try to follow an educational plan of action compatible with these needs.

Symbolic rewards and punishments exert control over behavior and these are learned. Students become extremely sensitive to the nodding head, the accepting smile, or the raised eyebrow. A teacher's unintended slur may trigger a vigorous emotional reaction (motivation) that dominates the student's thinking during this class hour and for the rest of the day. As values change, the symbols (gestures, words, dress styles, objects, etc.) that represent these newly acquired interests and motives come into existence and, in turn, run their course. Yet the social motives of individuals and groups are relatively stable and the discriminating teacher—especially if from an older generation—is advised to relate his teaching to these more enduring motives and to avoid the mod vernacular. This universe of discourse is far more transitory than the acquired social motives that are more similar than different from one generation to the next.

Complex behavior involves a *hierarchy of motives*. Students manage, with varying degrees of success, to attend eight o'clock classes. This achievement may be impelled, in part, by an immediate desire for a seat-next-to-a-seat, or even, perhaps, by a wish to understand the topic of the day. Behind these specific "eight o'clock" purposes the student is motivated to make a satisfactory score on the next examination or simply to achieve understanding at a level consistent with his aspirations. More remote may be his plan to meet the curriculum requirements and to emerge as a college graduate to assume his role as a respected and comfortable member of the community. Perhaps fewer students hold this final "ambition" today, but the hierarchical pattern of motivation remains as a distinctive characteristic for each student. In general, the biological needs are at the base while "self-actualizating" is in current vogue as the need at or near the top of the hierarchy. In between are many different motivating states and to Maslow, "A child cannot reach self-actualization until his needs for security, belongingness, dignity, love, respect, and esteem are all satisfied" (Maslow, 1971, p.

190). In effect, therefore, the motivation to learn a given unit of knowledge is partially dependent on prerequisite motivational states which may or may not be influenced by the teacher.

The relation between a student's *level of aspiration* when he starts a task and the quality of his performance has been the subject of considerable research. The findings show that rewarding "over" achievement (beyond a preset level) is more effective than to punish failure to achieve the expected level of performance. In practice, this means that the teacher should help a student maintain a realistic (reward-producing) level of aspiration. In a competitive situation among students with different intellectual abilities, the slow or weak students are especially likely to need this guidance and motivational support. A student's aspiration level has usually been linked with grades as the measure of achievement, but the status function of the grade-point average now faces strong competition. Ambitions are changing and aspirations heretofore bypassed or suppressed are surfacing as active factors in the direction and level of student achievement: participation in community "outreach" programs of tutoring, medical and legal-aid clinics, and youth counseling; independent study projects beyond the curricular frame; "underground" writing; prison reform; environmental reeducation in the community; "stepping out" of school for back-pack travel; consumerism, and the like. Some of these activities are consistent with the usual goals of education, others are not or, at least, not yet.

In Sum

Permissive acquiescence to student interest is, to some members of the faculty, a sign of weakness.

This defensive position misstates the instructional problem, since effective classroom learning depends on the teacher's ability to transform resistance to support and to maintain the interest and curiosity that brought students to his course in the first place. The task of stimulating students to productive academic effort is more difficult in a "required" course but, in any case, the teacher is part of the motivational picture whether he likes it or not. If the substance of the course is worthwhile, well planned, and if the teacher evidences an honest interest in the subject and the students, the problem of motivating students will almost take care of itself. Well-organized subject matter leading to relevant objectives and with constructive feedback along the way, does more to counter apathy, indifference, or negativism than do efforts to attack motivation directly.

Motivation, like learning itself, cannot be divorced from the individual person; self-esteem is an ever present need and especially so for the maturing young adult. The quest for self identity tinges nearly everything that students do, including their perception of teachers and how and what they study. The satisfaction of these self-reference motives is considerably more powerful than the various kinds of extrinsic rewards that are contingent upon the attainment of grades. A teacher's crutch-like dependency on extrinsic lures and threats for motivating learning ignores the intellectual curiosity of his students, their desire to understand, and their need for self-esteem. Conceptual ordering can be exciting and is most likely to become so when a student is free to seek information that will reduce his own uncertainties. If learning in college has been intrinsically satisfying, if curiosity has been fostered, and if students can confirm the social utility of knowledge, it is likely that questioning and searching will continue beyond the day of graduation. The ability to start this learning chain-reaction is one of the defining characteristics of a good teacher.

Chapter 6

Attitudes and Values Students Study By

Something has happened to the once docile student body that memorized what it was told to learn. For a time, new values surfaced to harry the academic sacred cows on the pastoral campus as students expressed the new self-consciousness of the counter-culture and the priority of humanism over materialism. More recently these protestations are muted as students recognize the personal and social implications of living in a scarcity oriented society:

> True, the youth leadership of the sixties generation has been all but eliminated as a cohesive force. This is a grave loss, and it ought to drive home the urgent need to find sensible means by which to induct young people into the exercise of power and responsibility. (Hechinger, 1973, p. 35)

Most schools have, in fact, made many changes toward better cohesion between the values of their students and the educational resources of the institution.

The Academic Climate

College students are still the cream of the intellectual crop and except for a few quivers here and there, not much has happened to the test-score profile of intellectual talent during the past fifteen years. Certainly the scholastic aptitude tests did not reveal the strong attitudes and values these students were bringing to the campus. The explanation lies elsewhere. The increase in college enrollments during the past twenty-five years "has flooded our campuses with students who represent an entirely new challenge to the . . . traditional concepts of liberal education. These students come out of different segments of society with different wants and expectations than our traditional curricula and organizational structures were designed to handle" (Brown, 1969). Students on the G. I. Bill following World War II set off the first shock wave and were followed by children from blue collar families and steadily increasing numbers of black students and the other ethnic minority groups. Education is now reshaping its instructional resources to meet the personal, social, and intellectual needs of this expanding population of college students.

This opening up of academia came at a time when the larger society was narrowing the range of options for the high school graduate and Kingman Brewster (1970) referred to the "involuntary campus" as one phase of the tight educational lock-step that predicates success in terms of continuous school from five to twenty-five. No wonder, then, that many students rebelled. They felt just as did a young man who told Brewster: "Like don't give me that stuff about how I'm here to learn; I'm here because I have to be; so if I have to be here against my will, why shouldn't I have a say in running the place?" Many of these students objected to being victims of a materially directed, success-oriented society which prevents realization of their deepest convictions about what is to be valued in education and in society. These attitudes are often expressed in high school and before; junior high schoolers (only four years from voting) along with those in high schools, are floundering as the college culture filters down to release strong convictions as to what education, authority, and life are all about.

During the past fifteen years considerable attention has been given to broad social-psychological factors that are now recognized as having such a marked influence throughout the college experience. Publication of *The American College* (Sanford, 1962) was a landmark analysis of the personal-social development of students. This report was followed by Kenneth Feldman's and Theodore Newcomb's (1969) review of the multitude of conditions leading to attitude change during the college years. They examined nearly 1,500 studies and reports covering the relatively stable forty-year period which *ended* in the middle 1960s. Taken in full scope, successive generations of college students seem to veer a little here and there but do not move off in new directions:

> Critical examination of several studies of freshman and senior responses to questions about their college experiences reveals that comparatively few changes occur in the personal characteristics of students and that even these few, while widespread among students on different campuses, are neither universal nor radical.
>
> Most conspicuous among them are a decrease in conservatism and dogmatism, an increased interest in intellectual pursuits and capacities in independence, dominance, and self-confidence, and a greater readiness to express rather than to inhibit impulses. (Newcomb, 1970, p. 1)

This important and detailed review showed that a student is more likely to be influenced by his friends and close associates than by cursory contact with remote teachers and passing acquaintances. Further, there is some indication that students are becoming less dependent on their teachers for personal or even intellectual support. But people, nonetheless, are important. From infancy, most of what a child learns is in an environment with other people, and as a young adult he learns to place high value on these interpersonal relations and the social codes of the group. Students treasure the company of their peers and if birds of a feather flock together, they seem to fly in tighter formation as they proceed through these formative years of college.

The experiences of home, high school, and community establish a pattern of attitudes and values for each student, and these influences converge in deciding which is "the best school for you." Ideally, the selection of where to go to college should match personal values with the "reputation" of a given institution. The public images of the Ivy League schools, the megaversities, the sectarian colleges, the "little Bohemia" liberal arts colleges, the commuter schools, etc., attract like-minded teachers and students. These values combine and interact to establish the characteristic academic climate of each school. Factors of reputation, public image, or academic climate are not, however, the deciding matter as to where most students go to school. Cost makes a real difference, and this means that most students stay close to home and, thus, the community college is vitally important. The academic climate at a commuter school may be different from that in a residential school but it is still an influencing factor in shaping the attitudes and values of its students. Most attention in the public media (and now in journals and books) to the student protest in the sixties was directed to the larger colleges and universities where a critical mass of students could be formed around the specific issues of the day.

The Humanistic Revival

The march on Mississippi in the summer of 1964 was an exciting demonstration of emerging student values. The Peace Corps was already a going thing, but it was tethered to policy-making in Washington rather than to the pragmatic idealism of the youth generation itself. Students were leaving the shelter long given by the campus to join a political revolution. Many of them had walked across the railroad tracks to the other side of town and found that society was, indeed, in a sorry state. The protest parade moved at a rapid pace from demands for racial equality and international peace, the values of the counter-culture, and on to the need for freedom to express one's individuality. On most issues the protesters stayed rather close to the college campus; students believed that the university could and should contribute to improving the human condition. As one boy said in his "letter from Mississippi" while debating the alternative of going back to school:

> Occasionally one gets very lonely down here. I go downtown and see the Illinois Central train which could take me all the way to Chicago. The idea of riding from here to Chicago is sort of strange. I could just get on a train, ride, and be back in a free country . . . I really don't know what to do. I'm going to meetings in Jackson next week with those interested in staying, but then I'm coming home for a while to decide. (Sutherland, 1965, p. 224)

What should he do? Continue his small but intensely personal contribution toward solving a vital social problem away from campus or go on to graduate work and a Ph.D. degree in the abstractions of a social science? In a sense, these student activists were liberals in the grand tradition of social reform: impatient, frustrated, and angry at the lack of progress toward values they held important. Most came back to the campus intent on protesting the inertia of education and government in adapting to change.

This outburst of social action upstaged the peaceful pursuit of knowledge for its own sake. The antiracial sit-ins and the anti-Vietnam teach-ins were evidence of only two of the many humanistic concerns of students and teachers sensitive to the discontinuity between the ideal and the actual. "Relevance" became the key word in the campaign for greater social pragmatism. The campus was not geared for this kind of action; it didn't even pretend to be action-oriented. Must every scholar and scientist also be a practitioner in his field? A strong argument can be made that the university should not become mired in the everyday workings of the principles and values it espouses. There are times in the life of a student when he will benefit by refuge from worldly turmoil; to pause and reflect and to seek clarification and perspective of both action and ideal. Well and good, but these well-formed academic values could almost be taken for granted, but should not the university also be a resource for social change? These students have probably made their point.

The Free Speech Movement at Berkeley in 1964 added a different theme to the humanistic revival— the freedom of students to express themselves, to do their own thing. The hairy head, the naked feet, and the decorations in between seemed foreign to the purposes of higher education, but the attitudes and values behind these "symbols" were, to many students, directly relevant to the educational directions they believed most important. The self-actualizing life style strains the scholarly and scientific habits of the cognitive-bound, discipline-bound professor. Like Narcissus in his final discovery of Goldmund (Hesse, 1931), students felt that the older teacher must learn to accept the validity of the "other path."

The question is not whether love, freedom, total involvement, and individuality are worthwhile ideals, but how can they be realized in an educational system so firmly rooted in extrinsic learning and the authoritative structure of class-conscious intelligentsia. The humanistic revival disassociates itself from an Establishment that determines its values by scientific and technical expertise and gross national product, and that continually seeks new ways to organize human labor according to the highest degree of efficiency and productivity. One of the strongest spokesmen states that nothing less is required than:

> . . . the subversion of the scientific world view, with its entrenched commitment to egocentric and cerebral mode of consciousness. In its place, there must be a new culture in which the non-intellective capacities of the personality—those capacities that take fire from visionary splendor in the experience of human communion—become the arbiters of the good, the true, the beautiful. (Roszak, 1969, p. 47)

No wonder such protesting shook up academia. It was, after all, attacking the high totems of scholarship, science, rationality, and dispassionate discourse—the prime criteria on which instruction, curricular planning, and academic achievement are based. Some comfort was found by counting noses and noting that only a relatively small proportion of students and teachers held a humanistically radical position. But polling statistics are hardly pertinent since they tell little about the direction of change over time in academic values. The pace of educational evolution is quickening but, obviously, students are not of one mind about love, spirituality, and Being rather than Doing; some protest against grading but are quiet about warring, others protest elitism but are quiet about sexuality. The college can neither ignore nor become captive to any one of these varying sets of values. The incomparable educational and social value of the principle of academic freedom should never be more jealously guarded by both faculty and students.

Institutional Adaptations

Over the years, the faculty has considered basic research, pure scholarship, and teaching to be its best means of serving the long-term benefits of society. But teachers also value individuality and the need for institutional adaptation to support this value among its students. In terms of total impact, the most important adjustments are those between the teacher and his students in individual courses throughout the campus. These specific adaptations are difficult to summarize since they are in response to so many different kinds of "pressures" from students, colleagues, and the community. Two institutional-level programs to gain curricular and instructional flexibility for undergraduate students are described here.

The Dormitory-Classroom Interaction

The college dormitory used to be a large hotel with small rooms guarded by deans of men and deans of women and supervised by counselors serving *in loco parentis*. Today, however, students are expected to police their own behavior and are less likely to be "busted" for reasons of personal conduct. They have gained access to an environment more compatible with their values of personal freedom and self responsibility.

The next step is educationally more significant: classrooms and living areas, traditionally separate in the university, are being integrated by bringing academic inquiry and study closer to the realm of the student's social and personal life. The Pilot Program at the University of Michigan (Hatch, 1972) illustrates the rationale and the operation of one such learning and living arrangement. When a freshman enrolls in the Pilot Program (despite the name, it is now over ten years old) he finds the following:

1. *Academic.* His fellow students in at least one of his classes are acquaintances from his residence floor or wing and, conversely, the dorm-room bull session is likely made up of students who have shared a common class that day. Many of the courses he takes are located within the residence hall and have been planned by students and counselors. Their clear preference is for the interdisciplinary, problem-oriented seminar—Nationalism and Imperialism, Alienation and Meaning, Literature of War, and Community—in which students study concepts related to their current living situation.

2. *Staffing.* In his residence hall the student associates with Resident Fellows who are graduate students selected expressly to function as "living-in" advisers but also as somewhat older exemplars of a serious commitment to the academic life. Although they are not expected to act as tutors or professional counselors, the "RF's" assist students with academic

problems and personal difficulties and spend a great amount of time in these various roles. Staffing Pilot houses with these able and recent veterans of undergraduate education is undoubtedly a critical factor in the success of the Program. Many of these advisers and teachers are members of the "new think" generation of graduate students who hold a variety of views on politics, social life, and individual values.

3. *Social activities.* Student participation is enthusiastic and widespread. "Alice's Restaurant" is more popular as a coffee house than it was as the dining room for the large dormitory—Alice Lloyd Hall. The Opinion Board serves as a central medium for the exchange of suggestions, petitions, or simply good ideas. In addition, outside speakers, visiting teachers, Free University programs (ecology, judo, modern American writers, etc.) are part of the daily scene in the Pilot Program. The climate has been described as intense, electric, and invigorating—productive educationally and socially.

There is no question about the Pilot Program's success. Three times more students apply than can be accepted and some observers have feared that vitality might be blunted by the large number of sophomores, juniors, and seniors who ask to stay on as participants in the program. One interesting measure of success is the simple fact that the furnishings, the equipment, and the decorations are protected and handled with care. The Pilot Program offers entering students personal involvement in a free and fluid environment; herein lies its appeal.

The Residential College

When a multitude of young persons, keen, open-hearted, sympathetic, and observant, as young persons are, come together and freely mix with each other,

> they are sure to learn from one another even if there be
> no one to teach them; the conversation of all is a series
> of lectures to each, and they gain for themselves new
> ideas and views, fresh matter of thought and distinct
> principles for judging and acting day by day . . . It is
> seeing the world on a small field with little trouble;
> for the pupils or students come from very different
> places, and with widely different notions, and there is
> much to generalize, much to adjust, much to elimi-
> nate, there are interrelations to be defined and con-
> ventional rules to be established in the process, by
> which the whole assemblage is molded together and
> gains one tone and one character. (Cardinal Newman
> quoted in Beard, Healey, & Holloway, 1968)

This insight by Cardinal Newman in 1852 gives
the rationale for a residential college. A number of
the larger universities have established residential
(cluster) colleges to reduce the impersonality of
numbers and to make programs more adaptable.
They seek to retain the best advantages of two academic worlds—the multitude of resources of the
large university plus the close accord between
teacher and student within a cohesive community.

A University of Michigan group (Newcomb,
Brown, Kulik, Reimer, Revelle, 1971) evaluated the
attitudes and values of students in the new Residential
College (RC) of this University. Applicants for admission were selected to make the RC student body a
representative sample of the larger number of students in the College of Literature, Science, and the
Arts (LS&A), namely, sex, in-state residence, and
scholastic aptitude. This allowed direct comparison
on many measures with a comparable sample of students from LS&A.

The first inventory of the attitudes of the entering RC class was made *before* these students came

on campus and the second round of data gathering was near the end of the first year. RC students spent a great deal of time interacting with their teachers and fellow students; they were sociable, well adjusted, and quite satisfied with the college experience. The authors interpret their findings to mean that:

> Although RC students were clearly more intellectually oriented than those in LS&A, they seemed to choose the RC not on the basis of its intellectual promise, but on the basis of its promise of psychological intimacy. The bright, intellectually-oriented students entering the RC in 1967 apparently expected to find congeniality, clarity of expectation, and fairness at a residential college, and saw residential education as an alternative to the relatively impersonal, competitive, and confusing educational experience at a large university. (p. 111)

A commonly cited truism of the college experience is that "students learn as much outside the classroom as they do in." What they learn, and how well, and from what source is less often specified. The RC evaluation study offers a partial answer since it was designed to assess changes in personal characteristics as a function of particular experiences in the RC program. Typically, student attitudes change over the four college years in the direction of more liberal political beliefs, less authoritarianism, and more independence of thinking. This trend also marked the first class of RC students. Especially significant were data indicating that, ". . . the initial differences in the attitudes and personalities of RC and LS&A students are *accentuated* so that the two populations become more distinct as they progress through college" (p. 114). The RC students changed more than did those in LS&A, which confirms the impact of an academic subculture in which there is community of shared attitudes and values.

Despite the social pressures for group conformity, e.g., to political liberalism, individuality was not submerged, thanks to the diversity among students, staff, and courses of study. Student opinions and beliefs fanned out in many directions, including the realization that RC was not the ideal setting for every student. Some drop out (from 25 to 33 percent) although attrition data are difficult to interpret since, sooner or later, many of these students transfer to LS&A or to some other school for specialized study. Also, some leave the campus for one or two terms as they seek a perspective on the meaning and values of education—another reminder of student resistance to the lock-step educational system.

RC costs the University more than Pilot Program but both are successful and these two "experiments" illustrate a direction of change in the curricular and instructional affairs of undergraduate education. In both Pilot and RC the sense of "community" is strong—the Pilot students asked that the course on community be represented in the core curriculum of its own program—a seeming paradox considering the high value these students place on independence of thought and action and their resistance to "required" courses. The same community theme occurs repeatedly in the Freshmen Seminars and informal discussion groups in RC. The influence of peers in the formation of attitudes and values is clearly seen in both of these units. The curricular arrangements show that the students are asking that their classes have value for their personal and social lives. They want to dig more deeply into "relevant" *problems* rather than be *exposed to areas* of subject matter and they actively participate as a standing curriculum-committee-of-the-whole. In fact, very few decisions are made in RC or Pilot without full hearing and input and vote from the students. The formal teaching-learning relation is less important than the living-learning process and this, of course, is the raison d'etre of these experimental programs.

The Commuter Student

Most college students cannot afford the high costs of residential campus living. As commuters they are transporting themselves to and from home or a job rather than mixing it up with their fellow students about the issues of the day. Their education is too tightly circumscribed by lecture notes, textbook assignments, and examination scores. The means should be found to compensate for the missing residential experience; the opportunity for a student to express his own attitudes and values and to assess those of his classmates. Rather than passively accepting the objectives, the instruction, and the evaluation of his teachers, the commuter student needs to become "involved" in the direction and the quality of his own education; he should be given ample opportunity to learn how to learn independently.

Leonard Quart and Judith Stacey (1972) describe the student-centered curricular arrangement at Richmond College (an upper-divisional unit on Staten Island of the City University of New York):

The Richmond College program is directed toward sons and daughters of policemen and construction workers and toward returning veterans of Vietnam. Its students have, by and large, been deeply conditioned to accept authority passively. Their homes, communities and schools—both parochial and public—have done little to equip them with self-confidence or a sense of individual autonomy. Thus they have not been prepared to assume responsibility for their own learning easily or to respect their own talents. (p. 15)

Behind the innocuous title, "Integrated Studies," a radical education revolution occurred and with predictable consequences. Some students stayed away from class entirely and a number of teachers backed off. Soap boxes replaced study desks for other students but through this turmoil the faculty could see that Integrated Studies was sharply questioning the methods of teaching, course content, and the coercive aspects of institutional life. Obviously educational change of this order does not come smoothly.

The responsibility for opening up the educational experiences for the commuter student rests sooner or later with the individual teachers in their own area of instruction—substituting group discussions for lectures, holding buzz sessions, offering independent study and tutorial options, forming special interest groups for evening activities, brown-bag noontime discussions, or sunrise seminars. These arrangements will usually be tied to the subject matter of a given department and the interests and values of its teachers.

Two examples illustrate the trend toward the more "open" classroom; an environment which encourages students to elect within-course options and to pursue problem-oriented goals in concert with their fellow students. Both of these innovations can be adapted to a commuter school:

1. One of our stereotypes of the history curriculum (more often wrong than right) is series of courses divided into chronological units. One offering on the "History of the American City" (Warner and Mann, 1972) carried an enrollment of approximately 300 students. An optional once-a-week lecture was available

but more often this session became an active discussion group as students came together from their prior involvement in small interest groups, or as a member of a field-work project team, or from independent study. The teacher and his assistants compiled bibliographies of topics identified by the students; topics that linked the American City to changes in the national economy, international migration, national migration, transportation, and the like. Students were free to identify themselves with groups of other students who shared similar interests and concerns. Students wrote papers, took tests, gave reports, and when needed, engaged in tutorial sessions with the assistant teachers. The key feature, however, was the freedom and the encouragement to follow and to express and, presumably, to modify one's basic set of attitudes and values as they related to the general area of the course.

2. The Bulletin Board curriculum, the Storefront classroom, Course Mart (Course Mart, 1972), etc., are variations of the Free University concept aimed at student participation and involvement in problems beyond discipline-bound conventions. Environmental Studies and Consumer Protection courses, for example, have been started by students as extracurricular, interdisciplinary (or nondisciplinary) ventures. Course credit may be earned since these offerings are reviewed and monitored by the usual faculty procedures for initiating new courses. Students, however, carry the major responsibility for setting up the course, carrying it out, and in assessing its personal and educational value.

Somewhere between the commuter and the residential student are those who live in private rooms, apartments, fraternities, and cooperatives. Wherever a few of these students are gathered, there might be a "classroom"; an interaction between students, information, and value-oriented problems. The logistical matters of who-pays-whom-to-do-what must be worked out, but questions about who proctors the final examination and gives the grades seem quite irrelevant in many of these interactive settings. Evaluation is intrinsic to reading and discussion and, when end-product reports are in order, peer judgments are valid and well received.

In Sum

Grumbling about courses and teachers and expressing feelings of unrest and stress are normal in the young adult. Students in the 1960s didn't like what they saw in the adult generation and didn't hesitate to show it. In response, the cozy, complacent snobbery of the cloistered school gave way to involvement with action-oriented knowledge; to bringing the educational resources of the nation to bear on the diseased condition of the world. Many on the faculty agreed, and changed what they taught and the way they taught to encourage each student to be curious beyond teacher-defined topics, to question educational orthodoxy, and to strengthen his identity with the problems of man and society.

Individuality does not lend itself to prescriptive treatment; it is nurtured when teachers and students respect and accept the differences that exist between them. The teacher facilitates student development less by lecturing than by the forthright display of attitudes and values which influence his own mode of thinking and action. What position does he take when analyzing the conflicts, the unknowns, and the tolerance limits within his discipline, and the dissonance between his discipline and society's use of it? Students appreciate the expression of such convictions but they are also sensitive to the gap between precept and example. They want to know what needs to be done to replace privilege with justice, bondage with freedom, and hate with love. Students speak of love without self-consciousness even though some of their elders wonder what this kind of anti-intellectualism is doing on campus.

Chapter 7

The Theory and Practice of Reinforcement

Psychology did not discover reinforcement or invent the term, and teachers have been meting out combinations of reward and punishment to students for hundreds of years and they will continue to do so, with or without formal knowledge of the principles of reinforcement and their relation to learning. Understanding these principles is worthwhile in its own right as well as for guiding the teacher as he adapts and reshapes the special conditions for learning in his course.

In essence, reinforcement means that a given response is strengthened (or weakened) by the consequence of having made that response. When a teacher says "correct" he is reinforcing a particular reply—returning evaluative information to the learner. "Wrong" is also informative although less specific. Thus, reinforcement can be positive or negative; as blunt as a kick on the shins or as subtle as a vocal inflection or a word not said. Every teacher is deeply involved in the conditions of reinforcement and implements this state of affairs nearly every time he meets with students or evaluates their tests, papers, and reports. The importance of reinforcement for college teaching should not be prejudged by text-book descriptions of salivating dogs, bar-pressing rats, and eye-blinking humans. These are laboratory arrangements used under precise condition to test hypothesis derived from theory. In its application to college teaching, reinforcement is managed in less obvious forms.

Reinforcement as a Principle of Behavior

The Greek philosophers and their successors have analyzed happiness, pleasure, virtue, and the Good Life. But reinforcement is more than subjective hedonism; it is a principle of behavior derived from scientific theory and empirical research. Early in this century (1911) the formal statement of the Law of Effect by the psychologist Edward L. Thorndike (1874–1949) gave learning a basic explanatory principle which bridged the distance between centuries of philosophical speculation and modern studies of behavior: "Of several responses made to the same situation, those which are accompanied or closely followed by satisfaction to the animal will, other things being equal, be more firmly connected with the situation, so that, when it occurs, they will be more likely to recur; those which are accompanied or closely followed by discomfort to the animal will, other things being equal, have their connections with that situation weakened, so that, when it recurs, they will be less likely to occur. The greater the satisfaction or discomfort, the greater the strengthening or weakening of the bond" (Wilcoxon, 1969, pp. 12–13). Stated simply, satisfaction, pleasure, and reward strengthen learning, whereas pain, annoyance, and discomfort weaken and retard the learning process. The Law of Effect (as the precursor to the principle of reinforcement) dominated the psychology of learning—both theory and application—for most of the first half of the twentieth century. It was the theory model for studies of praise versus blame, knowledge of results, and the relations between motivation and learning in the classroom.

Reinforcement Requires a Motivated Learner

Clark Hull (1884–1952) followed Thorndike as a leader in the development of formal learning theory as we have seen in Chapter 2. In Hullian theory, a need or "drive state" (motive, purpose, goal, aspiration, ambition) must already exist in the learner before a response can be *reinforced by virtue of its reduction of that need.* The efficiency of learning depends on the extent to which the responses being made reduce and satisfy the motives that initiated the learning effort.

Hull encoded the relationship between motivation and learning as a general principle of learning. Any object, event or situation can take on reinforcing value if it is associated with the reduction of a state of deprivation, that is, if it supplies a need at the time the learner is responding. The principle of reinforcement applies to the entire range of motivating situations—from primary biological drives to the rewarding effects of money, attention, approval, affection, and highly intellectualized social aspirations. The dependent relationship between learning and motivation is a familiar human experience but the explanation for this close relationship is now more clearly established than ever before by the hundreds of experiments on the motivational conditions that influence learning. The relationships between reinforcement and learning can be relatively simple and direct as in animal training, or as subtle as a vocal inflection in college teaching. Nevertheless, the principle specifies that (1) a need (motive) must exist before learning can occur, and (2) that which is learned must have been perceived by the student as reducing (satisfying) this need.

Reinforcement Is What Reinforcement Does

The application of the reinforcement principle to instruction is most clearly seen in the approach of B. F. Skinner (1953, 1968) and his analysis of behavior change. Skinner is a Behaviorist seeking to avoid two traps that he sees in most theories about behavior and human nature: (1) Speculative involvement about what goes on inside the organism and (2) an overdependence on . . . stimulus and stimulus manipulation. Skinner places emphasis on the response and its consequences as they occur in a relatively stable environment. In the typical Skinner-box for the study of reinforcement with lower animals, the hungry rat moves about until he finally presses on a bar that releases a pellet of food which thus reinforces the immediately preceding bar-pressing behavior. How do we know it reinforces? Very simply, because the rat more quickly returns and presses the bar again.

As in the laboratory, reinforcement is the crux of behavior control in the natural setting. This is where Skinner starts (and consistently stays) in his novel *Walden Two* (1948), and more recently, in his analysis of man and society *Beyond Freedom and Dignity* (1971). "Once we have arranged the particular type of consequence called reinforcement," Skinner remarks, "our techniques permit us to shape the behavior of an organism almost at will." The conditions for the control of behavior are right out there in front— the reinforcing effects of the responses made by the learner himself. No need, says Skinner, to speculate and to generate deep and penetrating theories about what is going on inside. The observable and manageable conditions are sufficient to establish the necessary degree of control over the learner. Reinforcement is defined empirically in terms of its consequences to the learner.

Conditions of Reinforcement

Obviously, some conditions are better for learning than others and the findings from research within and outside the laboratory detail the significant conditions for effective reinforcement. These offer a framework for the teacher who wants to emphasize the benefits of feedback information in his teaching plan.

Negative Reinforcement (Punishment)

Students learn about negative reinforcement (aversive contingencies) early in their school careers, and by the time they reach college they have developed a variety of devices to offset or avoid the teacher who relies on negative sanctions and punishment. Punishment often produces undesirable side effects of fear, embarrassment, frustration, withdrawal, hostility, rejection, and disappointment. A teacher who depends on punishment is almost bound to arouse negative attitudes in his students—a consequence that is unfair to the students and to the discipline. As every experienced teacher knows, punishment and its threat are relatively easy means of controlling students. But resentment, anxiety, and fear are debilitating—they inhibit positive action. Even boredom is punishing. When the student has reason to expect feedback, its absence can be punishing:

> No one continues to talk into a dead telephone; and amorous advances are more likely to be stopped

more quickly by apathy than reprimand. Yet students are constantly requested, even required, to respond in situations analogous to the dead telephone. Papers are handed in, experiments are performed, assignments are completed but from the student's point of view he might as well be dropping stones into a bottomless well—there is no reaction; his behavior is non-consequential. (Geis and Pascal, 1970)

Mildly aversive consequences may, on occasion, make a particular response more distinctive and when alternatives are clearly available, may redirect a student to forms of behavior that are more likely to result in positive reinforcement. Within the total sequence of day-to-day experiences, punishment or its threat may be necessary to help define the limits, the standards, and even the reward system within which teaching and learning take place. Punishment is misused, however, when introduced solely as a roadblock type of control in which behavior is halted without indicating the alternate routes that lead to positive reinforcing effects. Certainly, studying for purposes of achieving well-defined goals is generally more efficient and satisfying than studying to avoid negative consequences alone.

Schedules of Reinforcement

How often should a student be reinforced—after every correct response, on a schedule of time intervals, or some combination of these? The effects of different schedules on the rate of learning and retention can be dramatic. Elaborate systems of reinforcement schedules have been tested in the laboratory, and industry offers many examples of fixed and variable schedules of reinforcement—the weekly paycheck, the Christmas bonus, the "suprise" bonus, piece-rate pay, the sales commission, a raise in pay and the like. Similar patterns occur in schools—the fifth grader gets a star for every book he reads; the college student goes on the Dean's list when he earns a specified grade average; and a teacher's pay is raised when he receives another degree. As a source of evaluative information for specific learning, these are not particularly inspired uses of a reinforcement schedule. Various schedules of reinforcement have different effects on learning. Research findings show quite consistently that response patterns (habits) acquired under continuous (regular) reinforcement are forgotten faster than those acquired under an aperiodic schedule. Explanation as to why this is so is a matter of debate between theorists, but in practice, predictable regularity in teacher-to-student feedback may not be the optimal condition for learning material that is to be retained and used beyond the classroom situation. In any case, a good instructor helps the student avoid the dependent state of keeping his eye on the teacher for signs of either praise or blame.

The timing of reinforcement, that is, the time interval between a response and its consequence, is a special case of scheduling. For lower animals a delay in reinforcement usually slows down the rate of learning, but college students can bridge time by conceptually recreating the original situation and the reinforcing contingencies. Nevertheless, as a general rule and when other conditions are equal, reinforcement that follows a response immediately will have the strongest effect upon learning.

Primary and Secondary Reinforcing Effects

Food is a primary reinforcer to the hungry, bar-pressing rat, but he will keep on pressing the "clicking" bar long after the food stops coming. The "click" has become a secondary reinforcer as a consequence of being associated with food, the primary reinforcer.

The same thing happens to humans. A student may learn to like a subject he was not initially attracted to because the study of this material becomes associated with a strong reinforcing state of affairs, such as receiving personal attention from the teacher or recognition from his peers. The appeals that attract a student to a given field of study are usually replaced or supplemented by new sources of satisfaction (reward) as he advances in his field and takes on new responsibilities.

Intrinsic Reinforcement

Learning theorists, educational administrators, and teachers have developed considerable expertise in matters of extrinsic reinforcement. The personal satisfaction of acquiring knowledge and understanding for one's own purposes, however, is the more important aim of education. Insofar as independent learning is the ultimate goal of instruction, it is imperative that the teacher do what he can to help bring the reinforcing contingencies under the control of the learner himself.

"Self control" has never been an easy topic for psychology to analyze or to understand and, on the surface, would seem to be the antithesis of a behavioristically flavored reinforcement theory. Nevertheless, recent advances in research and theory extend this conception beyond the simplistic model of the bar-pressing rat or the pleasure-seeking human. W. K. Estes (1972), for example, points out that when the normal human learner receives rewarding or punishing consequences he also gains information and this *information* is more immediately the basis for planning a future course of action:

> In any choice situation the individual is assumed actively to scan the available alternatives and to be

guided to a choice by feedback from anticipated rewards. (p. 729)

Estes' "informational-feedback" theory bridges the empirical applications of reinforcement procedures with the self-directed processing of information by the human learner.

The difference between extrinsic and intrinsic reinforcement is illustrated by the research related to verbal learning. The programmed teaching machine, for example, was designed to optimize the contingencies for positive reinforcement by yielding immediate and explicit feedback. Later research and experience, however, have shown that a learner is not highly dependent on knowing *from an outside source* whether his successive responses are right or wrong. In a related area of research, students were asked to read textual material which included study-guide questions (without answers) before, after, or embedded within the text. It was found that they performed as well on later tests of comprehension as did those who were given *both* the questions and the answers to those questions. Learners in both groups, however, did somewhat better than the "control" learners who were asked no questions or who were distracted by irrelevant questions (Rothkopf, 1970). These findings indicate that programmed questions serve an attention-getting function as to what is important and they also alert the learner to decide whether or not he understands what he is reading. They help the learner become his own source of reinforcement. Many years ago, college textbooks used to carry questions along the margins of each paragraph. There is still reason to believe that this is a good technique for directing a student to the critical points in each paragraph, and to depend on the intrinsic reinforcement from the self-appraisal of how well he understands what he has studied. When a student writes a term paper or completes an independent study project, he has already experienced the major conditions of intrinsic reinforcement *before he turns the paper in.* Self-directed assignments of this nature help the student to make the transition from extrinsic, teacher-controlled, to intrinsic, self-controlled reward systems. The educational impact of the delayed feedback from the instructor, e.g., the test score or the course grade, is relatively minor compared to the self-reinforcing consequences of putting the document together. The intrinsic reward-value of learning is cumulative and if the student perceives his course of study as satisfying the motives for which he entered the class, then the process of learning will be both rapid and efficient and will carry lasting effects. The busy-busy or last-ditch efforts by the teacher to scurry about arranging external reinforcing contingencies are quite unnecessary if the content of study is worthwhile and if its sequential organization allows the student to evaluate his own progress.

Students learn from teachers—from hearing what they say and also from watching what they do. The teacher is a model from whom the student derives cues as to the direction and style of his own behavior. Bandura (1971) accounts for rapid learning in the natural social setting in terms of "vicarious- and self-reinforcing processes." The student receives vicarious reinforcement as he observes the feedback consequences experienced by his teacher-model. If he emulates this model, he is being intrinsically reinforced to the degree that he sees himself approximating the teacher's way of thinking, feeling, and acting. The student will be influenced (reinforced) more by a model he respects than by one he dislikes. The modeling influence of the teacher is far more pervasive than his narrowly defined role as an information giver or as a purveyor of the conventional norms and values of his discipline. Students also "read" the teacher in other roles—as citizen, parent, member of the academic community, and may pattern (reinforce) themselves along the same lines.

Specific Applications for Instruction

A number of teachers have developed specific arrangements to better utilize the principle of reinforcement when teaching large classes and to more directly involve the individual students in both the means and the ends of instruction. These procedures are among the more important resources for the improvement of teaching. In addition to the principle of reinforcement, these changes usually involve two other basic and significant conditions for learning: adapting to individual differences and specifying mastery of well-defined instructional objectives. These arrangements have been reported under various headings: contingency management, precision teaching, personalized system of instruction (PSI), self-paced supervised study, individually prescribed instruction, modular instruction, mastery learning, contract teaching and the Keller plan. The generic phrase "self-paced supervised study" seems to best represent the essential elements in this area of educational application. The development of a self-paced supervised-study instructional plan requires the teacher to come to grips with the instructional inadequacies, loose thinking, and informational gaps in their course of study. They are pressed into a rigorous, and sometimes sobering examination of their goals as teachers.

There is no single blueprint for redesigning conventional courses into the self-paced format but the first step, at least, is to organize the course into a number of semiautonomous (modular) subunits, e.g., one unit per week, or one unit per chapter, or in terms of specific bodies of information, procedures, or applications. This initial phase is likely to be a rather demanding task for the teacher, and one which demonstrates his understanding of how information should best be organized for learning. In many instances he may find it difficult to replace his accustomed lectures with resource materials for individual study (including supplementary study aids). In addition, a guide must be prepared describing the new procedures in considerable detail to forestall students' feelings of confusion and suspicion of this radical departure from the methods of teaching with which they are most familiar.

Normally a student will start with the first unit and proceed through an established sequence, although the modular units can permit variations from this sequence. When a student feels he has mastered a unit he is given an essay or objective test, or some other means of demonstrating mastery, depending upon the nature of the course and the preference of the teacher. This evaluation is often done on a credit/no entry basis, that is, failures are not recorded or held against the student. No "punishment" other than further study and testing until the student demonstrates satisfactory competence in the subject matter. Only then does he receive materials for the next unit. Thus, reinforcement is positive, specific, and continuous with each unit of study.

One interesting feature in several of these instructional plans is the use of undergraduate students as proctors, tutors, assistant teachers, mentors, and so forth. They may make the initial evaluation as to whether or not a student has passed the mastery test; they review performance and aid the student in his preparation for further testing or for advancing to the next modular unit. In most instances, these under-graduate assistants are selected from students who have taken the course. In this role they may replace the more expensive graduate-student teaching assistant and, where the educational benefits warrant, they can be paid in academic currency—the credit hour. Instructional participation by undergraduates is a significant aspect of these self-paced courses.

The senior professor in charge of a personalized instructional system is a very busy person. His carefully worked out study units demand constant revision for optimal self-study use by students for tutorial involvement by the proctors. Updating and reorganization take much more time than notes-to-oneself in the margin of course lecture notes. The "lectures," if any, are usually given as informal discussion sections or as the means to maintain and enhance motivation.

The course is completed whenever all the prescribed units have been mastered. Some students may finish the sequence of units in a few weeks, others may carry over into the following term. How should a student be "graded" when he has demonstrated mastery of the course content? In function, the grade is an administrative detail, since the educationally significant evaluations have already been made concurrent with the student's progress through the modular units. If required, students can be graded in terms of rate of progress: how long did it take to complete all the units, or how many units were completed within the academic schedule. Because of the wide variety of course designs, procedures, and evaluating arrangements, the teacher interested in considering such an adaptation for his own course should check the literature on this subject in his field or in a closely related area.

Courses with well-established domains of subject matter are most easily adapted to the self-paced arrangement. Joy Rogers (1972) has suggested that in survey courses, students be given the option of self-selecting a "menu" from an array of objectives. The option feature is appropriate for many liberal arts courses which have an open-end quality and in which students have some freedom to choose what to learn and also to select alternative means to achieve these goals. Obviously, the management of such an individualized study pattern for a large class would be quite demanding and would hardly be feasible without the participation of students as assistant teachers.

Judging by their favorable reactions, students seem to enjoy studying and learning under these self-paced conditions and there is no evidence that the amount of substantive information acquired is compromised by this method. Grade distributions do not offer meaningful comparison with conventional teaching, but no instance of inferior content achievement has, as yet, been widely reported (Kulik, Kulik, and Carmichael, 1973). These courses are sufficiently flexible to be adapted to a wide range of offerings for high school and college students and for the continuing education of the adult citizen.

Academia is not used to thinking along these lines and the charge is made that preprogrammed courses are shallow, superficial, empirical, and therefore deficient as to the demand for creative and insightful thinking and the drawing of value judgments. But would one claim that the large-class lecture can do these things? This personalized mode of instruction is to be defended and supported in view of its main features: logical organization of self-study units, explicit criteria of mastery, dominance of positive reinforcement over aversive effects, and flexibility with respect to individually different rates of learning.

In contrast to the teacher-centered lecture-testing mode of instruction, the self-paced arrangement gives the student far more freedom and dignity. He becomes a self-managing student rather than an echo of the teacher and the text. Professor Fred S. Keller is the author of the widely used format—the Keller plan—which he developed following his retirement from Columbia University. His enthusiasm and dedication to this form of teaching derives almost entirely from what he sees as its benefits to students:

> The world is going to see an enormous change in its techniques of education within the coming years, within the coming decade even. This change will not result, I think, primarily from automation, televised instruction, information theory, sensitivity training, miracle drugs, or the participation of students in curricular decision-making—whatever the values of any of these may be. It will come instead from the analysis of behavior, or if you like, reinforcement theory, applied to education, of which our plan is an example. This change will, I think, eventually maximize the pleasure of scholarly endeavor and occupational training, also increase the respect of everyone for such endeavors. Even, perhaps, in community living, for the old as well as the young, for women as well as men, for black as well as white, and for rich as well as poor. In our educational institutions, it will involve less emphasis on rigid time requirements and more attention to the individual, greater opportunity for success but with nothing provided gratis, more privacy for the person and less invidious comparison with others,

less competition and more cooperation with others,
and a greater respect for human dignity than has ever
been shown before in large-scale education. (Keller,
1972)

The Educational Control of Behavioral Technology

Reinforcement is, perhaps, the most significant single
concept from learning theory applied to education. It
is important because it simplifies our understanding
of how the learner benefits from the consequences of
his action and, thus, how he learns. Reinforcement is
neutral with respect what is "good" or "bad". The
moral judgment as to whether reinforcement (praise
and blame; carrots and sticks, reward and punishment) is well or poorly used is the responsibility of
those who decide in what specific ways students
should change.

The widespread use of this behavioral technology reminds us that Orwell's *1984* is not far away. A
moratorium on this powerful tool is not the sensible
response nor is suppression. It is important that
every citizen and citizen-in-training address himself
to the question: who shall control the controllers?
Who shall decide what knowledge is worth knowing?
In the last analysis, therefore, the value judgment has
to do with the goals of education in general and for
the individual student in particular. The technology
of instruction (or of testing, public opinion sampling,
sensitivity training, counseling, psychotherapy, and
the like) must always be evaluated in terms of the
uses to which they are put.

Chapter 8

Learning How to Learn (and Remember)

Learning is a continuous process of combining the familiar with the new. We learn how to perceive constancy in an ever-changing world of sensory stimulation, to perform old skills in new settings, to extract meaning out of new word combinations, and to solve problems, each of which is novel to some degree. Starting in kindergarten students have learned how to learn to do these things but not as well as they might, and this is why their education continues. During the process of his learning effort, the student acquires certain nonspecific skills—he learns how to learn. In the research domain, this important phenomenon has been referred to as the "practice effects" of learning.

Practice Effects

Practice effects are a normal component of a sustained learning effort and these effects (frequently a confounding variable, see pp. 21–22) must be carefully controlled in rigorous experiments on human learning. Experiments using animals must also control for these learning-how-to-learn practice effects. Repeatedly, for example, it has been observed that the early phase of animal learning involves a *nonspecific form of adaptation;* in effect, the animals must be "tamed" to the conditions of the experiment. Handling white rats for a few minutes a day helps their later maze learning almost as much as if they spent comparable time exploring the maze itself. Even faster learning results from a combination of handling the rat and allowing it to run down a straight alley from the starting box to the food box. Having learned that "if you keep on running you'll find food" the animal has acquired a nonspecific skill (a principle?) that can be transferred to different tasks. Animals learn other general guidelines such as, "don't retrace—there's nothing behind you that you haven't seen before, certainly not food." Harlow (1949) added considerable detail to the understanding of learning-how-to-learn with his studies on the acquisition of *learning sets* by monkeys (see Chapter 4).

Attributes of Practice Effects

The procedure for selecting Air Force pilots in World War II included six different 15-minute tests of perceptual-motor skills. The follow-up analysis showed that the validity of these tests lay mainly in the level of performance reached *during the first few minutes of each test.* Thus, the value of these "skill" tests was, more accurately, as a measure of how quickly young men could grasp instructions and adapt to the procedural specifics of a given task—how rapidly they learned how to learn.

In everyday experience we find that some persons in some settings seem to possess particularly well-developed "powers of observation." The ex-football player sees much more on the field of play than does his semi-interested wife; the park ranger sees much more on the nature trail than do his visitors; but these special powers of observation may not carry over to non-football and non-nature scenes. Learning-how-to-perceive (to observe) is a skill which improves as a consequence of practice in specific settings. With further and varied experience, this ability generalizes to a wider range of perceptual events.

Starting with the early experiments of almost one hundred years ago, practice effects were noted as subjects learned progressively faster how to learn the successive sets of verbal materials used in the studies. Verbal learning is essentially the process of encoding and actively organizing verbal associations into subjectively meaningful patterns. How fast the student learns and how well he remembers depends to a great extent on how well he has learned how to manage his own processes of verbal encoding and organizing. Memorizing is a cognitive skill which improves with practice but this improvement is linked to the kind of material being memorized and the way it is being learned. Experienced actors often display a remarkable ability to memorize the lines for a new play; they have learned how to learn this type of material, but they may be no better with telephone numbers than the rest of us.

Learning How to Learn in School

Two generalizations about practice effects, derived from research, can be used for application to instruction:

1. A nonspecific, general form of adaptation precedes and accompanies specific learning. "Getting in tune with . . ." and "getting rid of the anxieties . . ." "learning to cope," takes place faster with seniors than with freshmen who have had less practice

in acquiring the general, nonspecific learning-how-to-learn skills of being a college student.

2. Active participation on the part of the student is a necessary condition for practice effects to occur. He must read something and keep on reading if he expects to improve his ability to read. He must write something and keep on writing if he expects to improve his ability to write.

Freshmen have already learned how to learn, but not equally well in all areas. Some have specialized in mathematics, reading, or writing; some excel in sports or song, and some in gamesmanship with peers, professors, and police. The classroom instructor might list the skills of being a student as the ability to read books, take notes, answer technical and abstract questions, write papers and reports, and discuss worthwhile issues and problems, but many students are woefully lacking in these prerequisite skills for college-level learning. These students may have learned how to open their minds for informational spoon-feeding and how to earn a passing grade with a smile (or a tear), but many have not learned how to study on their own, or to read well enough to keep up with the class, or they are distracted from intellectual effort by an emotional disarray of anxieties, conflicts, hostilities, feelings of hopelessness, and so on. The instructional countermeasures to these deterrents to learning, or ways to improve the skills and personal attitudes that are prerequisite to learning how to learn effectively are considered here.

Study Skills

When a student asks "How can I study better?" he usually expects and is given a common-sense answer about the *mechanics* of studying. Fortunately, one of these—reading—is an ability that can nearly always be improved with specific training.

Reading improvement. Most college students are good readers, but even good readers find their skill inadequate in the face of the relentless pressure of long reading assignments. Faster reading speeds and greater powers of synthesis and interpretation of the printed page are nearly always advantageous. Poor reading is an obvious handicap; it can catalyze, if not assure, academic failure. Studies indicate that good readers tend to read more and are able to adjust their speed and their purpose; they have larger vocabularies and receive higher grades. Whether good reading develops larger vocabularies, or whether larger vocabularies tend to facilitate reading, or whether both are caused by a third factor such as general intelligence, are questions still largely unanswered.

Reading is a complex mental effort requiring a certain level of vocabulary. Good reading also requires a certain breadth of relevant background experience; the ability to comprehend what is read hinges on what the student knows, what he has seen, what he has experienced. Those with poor reading abilities tend to read all material at the same speed, whether for study or pleasure. They cannot move freely among words seeking the thread of an idea; they either read every word or they force-read for speed rather than for understanding. They are generally less able to apply what they read to ideas or situations beyond the printed page.

Increasing speed is not equivalent to increasing comprehension, although it may lead in that direction. With this warning in mind, most estimates show ordinary reading rates for college freshmen to average about 250 words per minute (wpm). Those who can read 375 to 500 wpm have reached a desirable level even though the material may be simple. Only rarely does an individual obtain a reading speed exceeding 800 wpm. There is as yet no conclusive evidence that faster readers comprehend more than do slower readers, except when elementary material is involved. In such subjects as science and mathematics, for instance, slow readers do as well as or better than fast readers.

Comprehension tests, too, must be closely examined before their results can be accepted. On some of the widely used and well standardized tests an intelligent student can obtain a comprehension score of 50 to 70 percent *without having read the material being tested.* Extrapolation from such scores would yield an infinite reading speed in words per minute!

Feeding into the misconception that efficient reading is equated with reading quickly, are myriad widely advertised reading dynamics programs which boast the secret of speed-reading. These panaceas often advertise their ability to double reading speeds in six to twelve weeks or to increase speeds to 1,800 to 3,000 wpm. They claim to achieve this phenomenal success by teaching the reader to read down the page, taking in large portions of a page in a single fixation. While it is true that students can train their eyes to move across the page more quickly, little attempt is made in these speed-reading programs to diagnose individual reading weaknesses and to specify programs which emphasize comprehension as well as speed or which carefully utilize the results of the full range of research on problems of reading.

Few students are unable to acquire adequate reading skills; many are not willing to go to the trouble; most are unaware of their deficiencies. Those who feel they read too slowly or at reduced comprehension levels can improve their skills by practice. Some will require the discipline and guidance of a structured "course"; others can manage on their own. If they feel their handicap seriously, they can move to remedy it.

Remedial instruction. A supervised program for improving study skills can be helpful if treatment is consistent with the actual need and if the student has the desire to improve. More often than not, the slow learner's handicap is a lack of interest, or a self-defeating attitude, or he senses an incompatibility between his personal values and those of his fellow students and teachers. His immediate problems relating to reading, note-taking, and paper-writing are likely to be symptoms of a motivational deficit that may have existed for several years. He has never really engaged himself in a program of study long enough for the "practice effects" to accumulate to a sufficient skill for learning as a college student.

Such students are often unhappy, confused, and discouraged, and they continue to engage in the defensive maneuvering they have learned through the earlier years of schooling. Their educational experiences have not been especially satisfying and they are now facing again the frustration of possibly not quite being able to make it. Inadequate prerequisite knowledge in a substantive field will, of course, hurt a student, but such a deficit is rather easily spotted and corrective action taken. Relatively few students fail for reasons of intellectual disability. The more likely reasons are such factors as a self-defeating attitude of indifference, negativism, and fear.

John E. Roueche and R. Wade Kirk (1973) examined several programs in remedial education in community colleges. Except for the bypass of the lecture mode, "No single instructional method was common to all the programs." To gain maximum student involvement various forms of self-paced supervised study were frequently used and tutoring and counseling were intrinsic to the program. The role of other students was particularly significant. "Often these older students have completed the developmental program and serve as living examples of successful students. These student tutors are peers; they understand the language, frustrations, and fears of the entering student and, perhaps most importantly, are able to communicate openly and honestly with him. A feeling of real trust is revealed by non-traditional students toward their peers who tutor them" (p. 67).

In many four-year colleges and universities, undergraduate students have demonstrated their value as tutors. They have fewer "bright student" hang-ups than do most of their professors and in addition to helping with course content material, they may help untangle the emotional confusions that frequently impede the academic progress of their peers.

Whether he be deficient for reasons of motivation, ability, study skills, or personal background, the poorly prepared student deserves as much attention from the faculty as the "honors" student. The instructional time and talent earmarked for the privileged honors programs could be more effectively redirected toward those who have not yet acquired the ability to comprehend quickly the meaning of what textbooks and teachers say.

Most teachers, however, have very few educational memories corresponding to the experience of the slow student coming in for "extra help." The teacher lives in a different motivational world from his "problem" students and may not sense the need for help as early as he should. Further, remedial instruction is not attractive to teachers; the academic bias is toward "bright" students who are usually much easier to teach, and who reward the teacher with high achievement toward the goals best appreciated by the faculty. A teacher's success in helping the slower learner should be recognized as a revealing measure of his competence as an instructor. Yet the prevailing reward system in research-oriented schools seldom recognizes the teacher who is willing and able to help the slower student.

Counseling the Distraught Student

At one time or another most students need a sympathetic ear, someone to talk to about their frustrations, anxieties, and disappointments, and also their hopes and aspirations. They need to affirm what is first and what is second and third in their personal scale of values. A student may seek out his teacher as one of the few adults in his environment whose judgment he respects and whose confidence he trusts. Thus, from time to time, nearly every teacher finds himself in the role of counselor, a responsibility not to be taken lightly. Effective counseling is difficult to achieve when the teacher is the one who defines the knowledge the student is supposed to learn and is also the one who evaluates the final level of achievement. Professor Edward Bordin (1969) has stated the task well:

1. Reconciling teacher and counselor roles.
   The fact that the teacher-counselor is also evaluator in the classroom may inhibit frankness. This is an inescapable feature of the teacher's counseling relationship as it is of his teaching relationship. . . . Evaluation implies authority which in turn can lead to resentment or acceptance, insecurity or security on the part of the student. The critical concern is not so much with authority per se but rather with the per-

ceptions of the use of authority on the part of student and teacher. It is at this point that the authenticity of the teacher comes into play. Genuine authority is more than a matter of status and the capacity to reward or punish. The student who perceives his teacher as being authentic, who respects his teacher, will be able to express honesty and trust and grow in the process. This is no less true in the counseling situation. . . .

The teacher as a counselor shares many pitfalls with other counselors. He may be overly eager to be helpful either to prove himself, to be liked, or because he overestimates the student's discomfort and helplessness. Others carry out too much of the authoritative teaching role. While there are many instances where correct information will contribute materially to the solution of a problem and while the perspective of an older person is useful, it is easy for the teacher as counselor to overestimate the importance of informing the student as compared to giving him encouragement and support in his efforts to come to grips with his dilemmas.

2. Some characteristics of good interviewing.

Many errors in counseling stem from a premature offering of information and advice. The counselor's interventions in the early part of an interview should be geared to (1) saying, and (2) questioning (not cross-examining) in an effort to draw the student out. Questions should stem from the student's stated purpose in coming and the content of his conversation and not from the counselor's particular interest at that point in time. The counselor should avoid asking series of questions or interjecting pointed, intrusive queries. Instead of "What is your major?" or "Why don't you study more?" an invitation to the student to explore an area of concern would be more helpful: "Let's look at what you hope to get out of college" and "Could you tell me how you go about studying?" Information and advice should only be given after making certain that the counselor has understood what the student is asking for and what his problem is.

The general guidelines above aside, good counseling does not lie in a mechanical application of rules. It rests in a genuine interest in the student which is reflected in the counselor's respect for the student's individuality, his special needs, and his right to accept or reject the information, advice, or assistance being offered. It rests in the counselor's ability to refrain from pushing the student into a preconceived mold or plan of action. It rests in the sensitivity that stems from being tuned in to the feelings and concerns often underlying the student's words and ideas. Such feelings as boredom, concern, anxiety, fear, and sadness are often revealed through subtle voice qualities, postures, and movements. Above all, good counseling is dependent on the counselor's ability to enjoy and care for the students coming to him. (pp. 3–4)

Remembering and Forgetting

Students often complain that teachers stress memory over understanding. But memory is prerequisite to thinking, the base from which thinking starts. The process whereby a student acquires, retains, and utilizes knowledge will continue to depend on learning, remembering, generalizing, thinking, problem solving, and kindred cognitive events. And, of these, memory is basic; the store of knowledge that is tapped for trivial recollections is also used for making wise decisions.

Theories of Remembering and Forgetting

No one method of teaching can be singled out as best for purposes of retention and no one theory is sufficient as an explanation for forgetting. Of the following three classical theories of memory, the first two need only brief mention since the first restates the obvious, the second has warmth and intrigue but is supported mainly by anecdote and case histories. The third rests on experimental findings and carries the weight of the argument in the present analysis.

1. *Forgetting through disuse.* For most people the cause of forgetting is uncomplicated: unused facts, ideas, and skills gradually fade with time. As a gross description of what happens, this is a reasonable view and its complement—that practice and review counter forgetting—is functionally sound. But the disuse theory fails to explain too many commonplace observations of remembering and forgetting. For example, why do some items fade more quickly than others and why do we suddenly recall names and other "forgotten" events? Information doesn't just peter out through lack of use; something happens over the passage of time. It seems more likely that forgetting is the result of active intervening processes during this passage of time.

2. *Forgetting as repression.* Forgetting as a form of repression (or suppression) is a theory widely held by psychotherapists. Even though disappointment, anxiety, and other affective states are important factors in cognition, this interpretation is not sufficient as a general explanation for all aspects of forgetting.

3. *Forgetting as the effect of interference.* The theory of *associative interference* holds that forgetting is the consequence of the normal activities of reading, listening, observing, and being intellectually awake and responsive to the concrete and conceptual worlds. It is a thinking man's theory since it is an account of acquiring, holding, and retrieving information, not feelings.

Forgetting is a function of time—not empty time, but time in which earlier experiences or current learning events have an interfering effect on the store of memory, an effect that shows up at the time of attempted recall. Over forty years ago it was demonstrated, for example, that college students forget more during an eight-hour interval filled with normal daytime activities like going to class, studying, listening, and talking, than they forget during eight hours of sleep. In other words, the kind of activity *between* the time of original learning and the time of recall is a major source of interference. There is a theoretical argument as to at what point during this interval is interference greatest. For practical purposes, the interference *appears* at the time of attempted recall and is presumed to result from the confusion, the intermix, between the new learning and the information in store. The folklore among students about cramming is soundly based—cram, then sleep, then get up and take the exam. Keep the interference between study and testing to a minimum.

A key element in the impairment of retention (forgetting) is the degree of *similarity* (real or perceived) between two (or more) successive learning tasks. For example, a student taking a Friday examination in Art History will more likely confuse the Monday and the Wednesday lectures if they were both on the Impressionists than if the two lectures were on quite different subjects. A second major source of interference results from the carryover effects of prior learning. It has been demonstrated rather clearly that future recall of what the student may now be learning will be less complete and less accurate because of the delayed interfering effects of prior learning. When the teacher attempts to debunk what students may have learned earlier, he is attempting to counteract this type of interference. Students come to Introductory Psychology, for example, with some rather strong preconceptions and the teacher tries to straighten things out, that is, to get the student to unlearn the "wrong" and then to learn the "right." Yet, even after a 50-minute lecture devoted to this purpose, plus outside readings, group discussion, and testing, the conversion may not be complete. The mixed-up state of information will show up on the final examination in the form of "poor retention." Interference has taken its toll.

Countermeasures for Forgetting

The interference theory has been emphasized here because it is supported by the strongest research base and involves the cognitive processes of acquiring and retaining information. Since it combines learning and memory, the efforts of the teacher to improve the conditions for original learning will, for the most part, improve the conditions for retention. The relationship is not isomorphic but it is, nevertheless, a relevant and useful guide—what is good for learning is good for retention.

Some degree of affect—liking, disliking; agreeing, disagreeing—is usually attached to what is being learned, and these positive and negative interests in a topic influence retention. One classroom-based research study showed that the degree of a student's acceptance of a given concept was a more significant factor than formal instruction in determining performance on a later content examination (Mikulas, 1970). In other words, these attitudes, biases, and preferences tend to filter in, or to screen out, certain kinds of information with consequent effects on the organizational pattern of what is being learned, remembered, or recalled.

Just as we tend to see only what we want to see, we also tend to remember what is most consistent with our prevailing interests, values, and prejudices. One doesn't "remember" to fasten his seat belt, he "learns" to give high value to this act. Allan F. Williams (1972) reports that, "81.5 percent of the children used seat belts when both parents did and were highly educated versus 3.1 percent who did when both parents had low education and neither used seat belts" (p. 5). One set of parents were "teaching" behavior control (as they did with respect to smoking, weight, oral hygiene, and the like) and their children displayed the retention effects of this kind of affective learning.

The "human element" of selective recall is a serious matter in a court of law, where unintended distortions of perception and memory may lessen confidence in the testimony of a witness. A student's struggle to remember may involve similar qualitative effects. He may "level out" an atypical event in his memory so that it fits his personal expectations and experiences. On the other hand, he may sharpen and exaggerate an item of particular interest out of proportion. Such qualitative changes in memory can be disastrous to the student taking an important examination which demands perspective and the scaling of priorities. To compensate for these subtle, subjective twists of memory and "unconscious editing" mechanisms, the student needs to develop a broader strategy of review than narrowly focused exercises in memorizing and drill. He should at least recognize, if not resolve, the marked conflicts between his own beliefs and values and those of the teacher who will make out the examination and evaluate what the student remembers.

Learning-how-to-learn and learning-how-to-remember follow the same course of action. Both are dependent on activities from which the learner, himself, gains understanding and meaning. Meaningfulness is the most important single condition to serve both purposes of original learning and retention. With practice—that is, with the opportunity to organize and to reorganize a personal and subjective network of verbal associations and images—the learner is building his own repertoire of basic skills for learning and memory (Kumar, 1971).

The teacher's task is to arrange conditions that will help a student to understand the meaning of the subject matter. Active participation on the part of the student is, for example, one of these conditions, since participation by way of writing, talking, or demonstrating a procedure carries with it many of the factors leading to good learning and retention. Attitudes and values have long retention; in fact, they stay in memory until replaced by new or rearranged feelings and beliefs. These affective states, therefore, have a strong stabilizing influence on the organizing associations that give meaning and coherence to information in memory.

The position has been taken that forgetting is the inability to recall. Information once learned stays in memory but we are unable to recreate or to recall the original material. Thus, it is evident that how much a student remembers depends, in part, on the methods and the conditions in which recall is attempted. A test of total recall, for example, places a more severe demand on memory than does a test requiring only that students recognize the familiar items. In other words, to pass a test calling for the recall of information—essay exams, fill in the blanks, the listing of items, etc.—requires a more thorough degree of original learning than if the same material is tested by recognition-type questions, i.e., most objective tests. The main difference between recall and recognition memory is the presence of cues in the latter setting which can be associated with the original learning experience. It is likely that most of what students learn will be retrieved in the verbal context of a recognition situation. In the search to recall the name of the person we see across the room, for example, we place him against varying backgrounds hoping to find some cues to reinstate the original introduction—at the office, at a social event, or perhaps at a professional meeting.

In sum, the best single answer to the question: "How do I improve my memory?" is to learn things well in the first place. Commercial courses on "memory improvement" basically offer special verbal and imagery devices to facilitate the organization and encoding of what is to be learned and remembered. The *intention* or *set* to learn for purposes of long-term retention is, itself, a helpful factor and if a learning objective is accompanied by the opportunity to organize the information in a personally meaningful way, the primary conditions are being met for good retention. In any case, learning how to learn and remember are general skills that the student must acquire before the teacher can help him learn how to think.

Chapter 9

On Teaching Students How to Think

The founders of experimental psychology were particularly interested in "thinking" and by this they meant the nature of conscious experience. In line with the reductionism of nineteenth-century German science, they introspectively examined mental activity in terms of its presumed basic elements: sensations, images, and feelings. They were forming a new Pure Science of the Mind, with cleanly marked off boundaries within the family of sciences. The pragmatic, utilitarian bias of America, however, required more from its psychologists than the introspective search for the structure of mental elements. The guiding question of the investigators in this country was to ask how the mind serves as an *instrument* for achieving goals and solving problems. Thinking was studied as a means to an end and became part and parcel of the generic domain of learning theory. In this context, our understanding of the nature of the thinking process becomes clearer as knowledge progresses about memorizing, discrimination learning, perceptual organization, concept formation, problem solving, and other basic components of "higher mental processes."

The following list of familiar words and technical terms illustrates the variety of research analyses related to "thinking" and are pertinent to teaching students how to think:

abstracting	discovery	originality
artificial intelligence	dreaming	planning
autistic thinking	gaming	problem solving
categorizing	generalization	productive thinking
computer simulation	imagination	reasoning
concept formation	insight	semantic general-
conceptual transfer	intelligence	ization
consciousness	invention	simulation
creativity	judgment	trouble shooting
day dreaming	logic and language	verbal mediation
decision making	modeling	

As an umbrella concept, "thinking" covers too much educational territory. Lumping all good things together makes it difficult to analyze and to evaluate the specific abilities of students and the effects of different methods of teaching. This chapter, therefore, will analyze certain attributes of thinking before attempting to tie things back together at the end.

The Psychometric Short-Cut

With the development of group-testing techniques (in World War I) the way was opened to measure the "intelligence" of all students as soon as they were old enough to read instructions and write answers to questions. At the college level, most of the larger schools established "testing bureaus" staffed by technical specialists. During the 1950s the domination of selective admissions testing increased to the point where most of the entering freshmen at a number of prestigious colleges scored in the top ranges of the national norms and most had been "straight A" high school students. Test-taking prowess is just one of the factors leading to successful academic achievement, but the easiest method of "teaching students how to think" has been to select brighter and brighter students and to define thinking in terms of what these students do. This self-fulfilling illusion continues as the institution and the faculty interpret postgraduate success to be the result of the intellectual impact of the curriculum, the institution, and especially their own influence as teachers. Skinner (1968) is caustic about this kind of confounding:

> If we throw a lot of children into a pool, some of them will manage to get to the edge and climb out. We may claim to have taught them to swim, although most of them swim badly. Others go to the bottom, and we rescue them. We do not see those who go to the bottom when we teach thinking, and many of those who survive think badly. The method does not teach; it simply selects those who learn without being taught. Selection is always more wasteful than instruction and is especially harmful when it takes its place. Schools and colleges have come to rely more and more on selecting students who do not need to be taught, and in doing so they have come to pay less and less attention to teaching. (pp. 118–19)

Skinner may have overstated the case, but not without cause. Colleges have leaned too heavily on the convenience of psychometric assessment without a corresponding effort to analyze and to evaluate the specific role of the teacher and the quality of the curriculum. The impact of good teaching is, itself, too important not to aggressively search out and develop better methods of teaching students the basic skills that combine under "thinking."

Creativity

Creativity is a magnetic word that attracts other words, i.e., a student enjoys a creative *learning experience* under an *innovative* and *imaginative* teacher.

Words like these offer few handholds for study, and researchers have tried to shed light on what "creativity" means. Three different methods of research analysis—psychometric, personality assessment, and experimental—will be briefly considered here.

The upsurge of psychometric research started with a paper by J. P. Guilford (1950) in which he questioned the assumed high correlation between intelligence and creativity. In successive reports, Guilford drew the important distinction between divergent and convergent thinking which, loosely interpreted, is the difference between open intellectual searching and closed intellectual ordering. Guilford (1959) has characterized divergent thinking as being fluent and flexible in comparison to the more integrative and focused responses to a problem situation. This distinction reflects the different kinds of tests Guilford developed in his analysis of the "structure of the intellect."

A number of different investigators have confirmed that within a given range of intelligence, such as the college student population, the correlation between I.Q. and presumed measures of creativity is low. On the other hand, when a wider I.Q. range is sampled, bright students are more likely to demonstrate creativity than those from below average levels. The psychometric analysis is constrained by the culture-bound quality of the diagnostic and measuring instruments and conclusions about the relationship between intelligence and creativity must be tenuous until the measurement and criterion problems have been worked out. If, for example, a school wants to select highly creative students, there is as yet no consensus as to what an appropriate test would be like nor is there agreement about the criteria that distinguish creative from noncreative products or performance.

A second methodological approach involves assessing the personal characteristics of creative people. Ann Roe (1943) gave impetus to this approach with her in-depth studies of highly productive scientists. Among other things, she found that these creative persons worked very hard during both the long periods of preparation and the execution of their projects. More recently, Barron (1969) selected participants from fields of mathematics, creative writing, and architecture who lived together for three days in close social interaction with the "experimenters" and with one another. The results indicated that such persons quite consistently showed strong individuality and independence of judgment. Rather than being emotionally disturbed (the "mad genius" stereotype), the creative person was well organized and flexible but, above all, he was independent.

The experimenter faces the same problem as the teacher: how to define, to generate, and to evaluate creative behavior. Most of the experimental efforts to increase creativity seek either to encourage independent thinking, to increase the frequency of uncommon responses, or to generate new combinations of ideas. In the typical experimental approach, a subject is shown an abstract drawing, for example, or a picture of an object and is asked what it is, how it might be used, or what he associates with it. More specifically, a laboratory experiment is usually designed to test a particular hypothesis relating to some aspect of creativity. In one study (Maltzman, 1960), subjects were repeatedly presented with a list of stimulus words and required to give different responses to each stimulus. As stimuli recurred, the responses became more uncommon. Later, when presented with new stimulus materials, the practiced subjects offered more original responses than untrained subjects. This type of training in "originality," however, did not seem to affect performance on other tests of creativity.

The classroom is not normally the site where creative and original responses are best appreciated. The atypical response can upset a class unless, of course, the group is purposefully *brainstorming*. In this process a group generates as many ideas as possible, withholding criticism so as to encourage free-ranging ideas. Maier (1971) finds that group discussion can be managed for large classes and that, "through interpersonal conflict, participants learn that controversial matters not only have two sides, but that cooperative exploration of both sides of an issue often suggests new [creative] alternatives." (p. 724)

The distinction between creative and noncreative problem solving (if there can be such a distinction) may be more cultural than psychological. Changes in popular taste may elevate a work of art from obscurity to the status of a creative masterpiece (although it may later go back to the museum archives). The history of art and music and literature is replete, not only with creative geniuses who were ahead of their times, but also with youthful prodigies who later faded into "mediocrity." Society can be a fickle judge, but a decisive one where the criteria for creativity are concerned.

Formal educational programs designed to "teach for creativity" may be successful now and then, but convincing generalizations as to exactly how this teaching should proceed are limited. Until some agreement is reached as to whether creativity should be studied as a process, or considered only in terms of the product, or at the opposite extreme as a subjective experience, the teacher might best leave creativity unregulated and simply accept and appreciate its spontaneous display when found. Learning theory is more at home with "problem solving" and views creativity as its romantic counterpart.

Concept Formation and Problem Solving

Man can respond to stimuli as *symbols of something else* and this fantastic ability for manipulating abstract ideas gives him a degree of freedom from the limitations of time and space. In preparation for the future, he forms concepts and principles that emerge from his review of past solutions and the experience of others. Man's ability for conceptual learning is his strongest resource for adaptation and, thus, the most important intellectual resource for his education.

Concept Formation

In the problem-solving sense, thinking starts when our habits and attitudes fail to resolve conflicts or to remove obstacles. Normally, our repertoire of verbal, conceptual, and attitude stereotypes is sufficient to take us around and over most problems. Many of the high-sounding and insightful statements that appear to "solve" a problem are simply dressed-up expressions of tightly held prior beliefs and well-practiced ideational habits (concepts). Good or bad, thinking involves concept formation.

A concept is an idea with a label and the forming of concepts and their application constitute a major part of what college students learn to do. Sometimes concepts are stated formally as in a principle of science, or informally as in a humanities discussion. An outline of a course is often mainly a listing of the major conceptual categories making up a particular area of knowledge. The meaning of these concepts is supplied by the learner as he integrates the old with the new and reorganizes his base of understanding—he is "thinking" about the subject matter. A young family of five, which included two adopted black children, was described by the three-year-old genetic white child as "two brownies, two whities (self and mother), and one spotted" (her freckled father)—a quite satisfactory set of conceptual categories as differentiated by the child. Each person's conceptual system serves as his means for tying together the constantly changing sequence of specific and concrete experiences. This is as true for the child as for the scientist, the difference being the number and the complexity of the conceptual categories.

Concept labels are applied to a class of stimuli with common characteristics. As a child proceeds through school, his concept learning becomes more complex to include open-ended ideas for which finite meanings are as yet unclear, such as freedom, individuality, justice, patriotism, and humanism. College-age students have the brain power to acquire, retrieve, and utilize abstract concepts. This, rather than their ability to memorize, is their distinctive talent. It follows, therefore, that college instruction should be oriented toward the learning of abstractions—concepts, principles, generalizations, and values. Courses composed of descriptive storytelling or memorized recitals grossly underuse these intellectual capabilities.

The basic conditions for concept learning can be studied in the laboratory. A typical task involves sorting a deck of specially prepared stimulus cards into, for example, different conceptual subsets based on specified relations of: color, design, number factors, and type of border. These concepts lack the content complexity of a "natural" concept but can be made into quite a difficult "thinking" task depending on factors such as: the number of relevant attributes, the dominance of the attributes, the number and proportion of positive and negative instances, and how much information the subject is required to keep in mind. The research findings suggest certain procedures for teaching concepts.

A student can quickly become lost in a maze of conceptual attributes that confuse rather than combine toward the formation of a meaningful principle. When this occurs, direct instruction can turn a student's attention to the relevant attributes. Mushroom hunting, for example, may be a chancy hobby but one which can be made quite secure through concept learning—by learning the attributes of poisonous species. The teacher should be firm, direct, and clear about the distinguishing features, for example, of the deadly *Amanita verna*. After the four attributes of the Destroying Angel have been pointed out, the important part of concept learning continues as the student attempts to classify further positive and negative instances of edible and nonedible mushrooms. These discriminations between confirming and nonconfirming instance should be practiced and tested in the context of new items, situations, and events. Students sometimes memorize the attributes but are unable to verbalize the controlling concept. "I have a hunch" or "My intuition tells me . . ." may be a quite satisfactory "sensing" of the significant relationship—with or without the correct symbol-label.

Students differ from one another in the strategies they prefer in concept learning just as in other kinds of learning. Some, for example, prefer to keep the big picture in mind and proceed to form a concept against this total gestalt. Others focus on a particular attribute or they may generate a specific hypothesis and test its worth against the successive instances that they encounter in their reading, laboratory or field work, or in the clinic. Concept learning nearly always involves a certain amount of heuristic exploration and these subjective variations in associations, organization, and strategies make it difficult, for example, to write an efficient computer-based program for teaching abstract concepts. While students like to know what leads to what, they also find that some ideas come as a flash of insight, a discontinuous jump from a period of preparation and exploration to the final grasping of the meaning of the concept itself (sometimes called "discovery" learning).

Concepts better serve the problem-solving purpose than do rote memorized facts. An expert troubleshooter, for example, tests one idea against another in making a diagnosis of the malfunction in the machine (in the person, or in the society). The problem-solving contribution of a concept, however, is lessened when its cognitive meaning narrows down to a verbal stereotype with heavy emotional overlays. These affective components tend to "take over" as factors controlling when and how the concept is used. Concept labels carry connotative as well as denotative meanings and these are displayed to the point of distress in international name calling, educational polemics, and religious exhortations. Political appeals are laced with concepts that have acquired stereotyped, affective meanings (rhetoric) that sway opinion and voting (lever-pressing) behavior.

Thinking—as in the Process of Solving Problems

In *How We Think,* John Dewey (1910) set forth his now well-known steps in the problem solving process (modified slightly):

1. Recognizing and defining the problem
2. Forming best guesses about possible solutions; clarifying the alternatives and the options (the hypothesis stage)

3. Gathering data, information, subjective analyses, and unconscious reordering (the incubation stage)
4. Drawing a conclusion; confirming or denying the original hypotheses
5. Utilizing, applying, and forming generalizations

The fact that this five-stage sequence has survived repeated analysis and testing by educators, scientists, scholars, and professionals confirms its essential validity. While it doesn't explain how problems are solved, it does aid one's orientation as to where he is and what should happen next. It is sometimes difficult, for example, for a faculty-student committee to make progress until the preliminaries are over and they agree on how to define the problem, and the steps to be taken toward their common goal.

Many course offerings list "problem solving" as a goal; to teach students to think as a (chemist, biologist, engineer, etc.) thinks. This can be a mere dodge to avoid being responsible for specific objectives, but when not thus abused it is an excellent instructional objective. If the teacher can clearly set forth the logic and the step-by-step *processes* that mark the way he and his colleagues think, he is, in fact, providing a top-drawer instructional unit. As students proceed through the assignments of the course they acquire definable skills relating to the techniques and the principles of problem solving within a prescribed area of knowledge. The transfer value of this type of understanding is very high indeed.

In his Millikan Award Lecture, John Fowler (1969) made a strong case for a new orientation in science teaching which would give specific emphasis to the *process* by which new information comes about, how problems are attacked and how solutions are tested and then generalized to new situations. He pointed out that physics teaching traditionally includes content objectives as well as process objectives—the latter being concerned with understanding and being able to demonstrate the methods of physics as a science; the processes by which problems are solved. "But if we play from strength and relegate most of content teaching to text and its natural extensions, then we can attack the more difficult problem of teaching process" (p. 1199). This emphasis applies to the course for nonmajor—as well as for professionally-oriented courses since, in either case, the value of a course lies in the generalized transfer of what is learned. Teaching students how to think means, in physics, preparing students to make decisions relating this science to new situations and to "critically analyze a new scientific argument."

The existence of a problem, like beauty, is "oft in the eyes of the beholder." The purpose, the intention, or the *set* of the problem solver must be taken into account, for despite its apparent trial-and-error randomness, a student's search for a problem solution is usually purposeful and connected. In cognitive theory (see Chapter 2) successful problem solving results from restructuring the perceptual and cognitive relations between the "figure" and the "ground"—the problem object within its setting. The "Eureka" experience is an illustration from history of this kind of sudden understanding. The many studies on "functional fixedness" (perceptual habits) demonstrate how difficult it is to change customary ways of searching for and "seeing" the means to solve a problem. These studies show how a pair of pliers, for example, cannot quickly be perceived to function as the weight for a pendulum, or a small box of carpet tacks will not immediately be utilized as a candle holder (when the subject is given the task of finding one). The problem results not from the lack of information but from perceptual and cognitive rigidity; we bring a habitual *set* to the problem situation and are slow to change.

Two stimulus-response experimenters (Glucksberg and Weisberg, 1966) offer a different interpretation, namely, functional fixedness is less a matter of perceptual reorganization than the lack of an appropriate verbal response for the problem at hand. They found, for example, that if a box of tacks were simply labeled "box" rather than "tacks" their subjects could invent a candle holder more quickly. When students acquire a vocabulary about problem solving in a given area, they are forming a verbal context within which they will more likely find the means to identify the critical relationships that constitute the "problem."

The cognitive and the stimulus-response theorists differ in their explanations of *set* but agree it is a factor of major importance in problem solving although their research does not indicate direct and effective modes of application. Some general suggestions follow from studies using anagrams, where it was found that the most effective learning sets result from the combination of a moderately high degree of learning on a single problem *plus* exposure to, and practice on, several different kinds of similar problems (Morrisett and Hovland, 1959). In other words, and as a guide for the teacher, a mix of both intensive and extensive training, depth and breadth, seems to be the best preparation for later engagement with a different sequence of problem-solving tasks.

For the most part, the gap between theory and application is filled in by way of exhortations such as "shift your set," "change your mind," "think of new approaches, combinations, and relationships." Advice-giving of this sort is not a particularly enlightened mode of instruction for long-term benefits. More than anything else, students need practice in solving problems—and especially the opportunity to analyze the nature of problems and to conceptualize the procedures leading to their solution—the logic of the problem-solving process. The instructional use of simulation and academic games is an effective means for giving students repeated involvement with the significant decisions leading to problem solving.

Simulation and Decision Making

Simulation makes it possible to recreate critical problem situations in which students revise their judgments as the consequences are known. They can practice and apply their best thinking in the reaching of decisions. Simulation is a planned arrangement to duplicate *certain* features of the physical, social, or conceptual environment and to represent these selected parameters for student manipulation and control. The first requirement for developing a simulation exercise, therefore, is a clear blueprint of the essential features of the task to be accomplished, the problem to be solved, or the decision to be reached. Only when these performance requirements are specified can a simulation-training program give students the opportunity to exercise decisions that are important and necessary for in-the-field performance.

The second requirement for good simulation calls for active participation rather than passive observation; each student has some degree of control over the sequence of events. Students manipulate the device or review the data and become directly involved in the decision making and the course of action carried on by the simulation. In some situations the teacher can write himself into the simulation in a particular role such as an evaluator, referee, communicator, or as a source of informational "noise."

The third critical element in simulation follows almost automatically from steps one and two, namely the return of information to the student regarding the consequences of his action, his decision, or lack of same—feedback, knowledge of results, reinforcement. The return to the student of evaluative information is the basis for making corrections or to go on with further decision making.

Medical diagnosis is a form of problem solving and the computer-simulated patient allows medical students to practice diagnostic decision making about well-marked disease syndromes. Similar training arrangements exist in education, business, city planning, and in many disciplines. Perhaps the most extensive and impressive single program is at the Manned Space Craft Center in Houston. Space research offers a good example of "teaching people how to think," that is, to make fast and accurate decisions in the solution of problems. A major segment of the resources of the Mission Control Room is directed toward executing simulated missions in which one emergency is piled on top of another. The ground controllers of space flights practice and improve their reactions to the rapid and complicated sequence of informational inputs and rehearse the pattern of decisions for controlling the mission and the life of the astronauts in space. Nearly every conceivable aspect of malfunction or breakdown from computers to people is tested and practiced to the point of maximum operator efficiency, accuracy, and dependability.

Gaming differs from simulation in that the student is directly involved with the conceptual dimensions of the subject matter; the decisions follow logically from the theoretical model. Tic Tac Toe is a relatively simple game; checkers is more complex, and chess even more so, but the tactics and strategies for playing these games carry little transfer value for decision making and problem solving beyond each of these particular games. Monopoly is a simplified example of a business game in which the rules are quite specific to the game-board situation and where the payoff is winning the game rather than being able to verbalize strategies dictated by principles derived from an economic model.

Wiff 'n Proof (1962) and Queries 'n Theories (Allen, Rugel, and Ross, 1970) are two examples of games designed to teach students how to make and to manage decisions involving symbolic logic and how to organize, analyze, and synthesize scientific data. Their educational value derives from the substance of what is learned, not from mind stretching exercises in and of themselves. Thus, academic games are designed to teach students particular concepts, procedures, and logical relations that are intrinsic to a given subject matter, and the student is expected to demonstrate his understanding of certain principles basic to the area. Gaming is a form of controlled and directed problem solving that involves the transformation of laws and principles from a theoretical model to application. An instructional game requires that the student, whether the winner or the loser, carry away from the game a better understanding of the concepts derived from the basic model and represented in the procedures of the game.

People differ in their risk-taking characteristics and in the value they assign to the different "input" variables in a decision-making situation. Simulation and gaming provide a means for observing and comparing the effects of subjective preferences when selections must be made from the available options and when a judgment must be given as to the consequences of each decision. This is the human element that makes decision making so difficult. Thinking can rarely be separated from the emotions—the subjective preferences and values of the thinker.

Gambling is a form of competition between one person and the odds given by the dice, the cards, the horses, and so on. The participants reveal their personal values—the subjective utility—via the odds they select in placing their bets. In contrast, consider what happens when two or more persons play an instructional game related, for example, to mathematics, business, economics, city planning, ecology, or international relations. The subjective utility factor is here intermixed with the more purely rational elements designed into the game. The results can be psychologically quite interesting although it may be difficult to untangle logic from impulse, fact from fancy, knowledge from illusion, and skill from "chance." Obviously, these subjective factors increase the complexity of a "rational" game and also the difficulty of defining the criteria for evaluating the educational impact of these games on students— are they learning to control their thinking or their feelings?

Because simulation is under less rigorous restraint from a conceptual model than is an academic game, the instructor can more easily adapt simulation to represent attributes or conditions that are important for students to understand. Once "set," however, a simulation exercise, or a game, may drift into a sequence of mechanical operations. They need to be revised and updated to assure that students will be engaged in making decisions relevant to a problem rather than memorizing the sequence of "steps" in a contrived and artificial procedure.

A Student Can Only Think for Himself

Teaching students how to think is asking for trouble. Habit produces conformity and predictability, but thinking produces diversity, nonconformity, and challenges not anticipated by the teacher. In the traditional liberal arts institution, thinking (like justice, truth, and love of country) was an articulated ideal, although its actual practice was often by chance, by pranks, or by finding ways to bypass institutional authority. Students were set to the task of memorizing knowledge and the memorizing process, per se, was valued over the factual, conceptual, and methodological content of what was being learned. Students were herded sheeplike through a curricular corral and into shearing sheds where the wool was graded, not the student. Fewer colleges continue on this misguided course, but education is still widely conceived as an arrangement to give information to students who are expected to give it back (students say "regurgitate") to the teacher on quizzes, final tests, and comprehensive examinations. This kind of mental exercise is not very high-level thinking and, further, it is assumed that the information given is the kind of knowledge on which a student can stand secure for many years to come. Such a stable informational state is no longer the case, if it ever was. George Katona (1969) describes a better alternative:

> There may have been a time when professors and experts "know the answers," [but] it is no longer possible to teach that "This is how it is." The teacher cannot say, "Learn this by heart, then you will be an expert." . . . The function of teaching—at least beyond some minimal level—is not transmission of information. The teacher must find a way to motivate students to strive for understanding. The major task of students is to learn how to learn. One important avenue of such learning is to follow the development of new ideas, that is, to understand why research is undertaken, how it is done, and what its results are. This

may often be learned from secondary sources. Yet the experience of associating with original researchers and their ideas represents one of the best ways of learning. (p. 6)

A good instructor need not be a "leading edge researcher," but as a consumer of contemporary research, he can update the curricular substance of his course more quickly than textbooks can be revised. Facts, methods, theories, and attitudes constitute the content of a course of study and are, therefore, the tools with which a student thinks. If these are out of date or limited to the teacher's personal biases, the student's thinking will either be off target or inadequate to the transfer tasks he will later meet.

Teaching students how to think is done by precept and by example. The teacher provides an informational base for learning, but he also models values which students may incorporate into their own thinking. Value judgments that hold up over time and with different people, places, and events, are the essence of good thinking and the test of wisdom. To help students achieve the ability to make these judgments is a teacher's most demanding challenge. In a sense the teacher is an agent of society, the mediator between the accumulated knowledge and norms of a culture, and the abilities, expectations, and aspirations of each student. By accepting and learning to encourage diversity, and by freeing his students to acquire distinctive attitudes and different beliefs, and to test new ideas, the college instructor teaches his students how to think and how, thereby, to become a dithering influence within a discipline specialty or on an otherwise complacent society.

Chapter 10

Person to Person Interaction in the Classroom

A two-person tutorial session is a social group and so is a large lecture class. In both these groups and in the many other kinds of instructional settings, successful teachers are those who are able to utilize the dynamics of the group for the achievement of course objectives. These intragroup processes have been studied extensively in both theoretical and applied research as investigators have examined how groups are formed, how group norms are set, how groups function, and what factors lead to group disintegration. In the educational setting these studies analyze the interactions between the personal characteristics of students and teachers, the influence wielded by one's fellow students, and the impact of the institution as a whole on these relations. Research on the interactive processes within and between social groups is as relevant to teaching as is research on learning or on particular teaching procedures.

A teacher defines his social role in the class, on campus, and in the community, in part, by what he believes is expected in light of the "traditions" of the local institution. This intellectual-social-cultural environment has been surveyed, probed, analyzed, classified, reclassified, and assessed as different investigators have sought to determine more exactly how the campus environment influences students. This area of research and development is fairly broad gauge and is more directly applicable to the sociology of higher education than to the psychological interactions between a teacher and his class and among the students themselves.

The Climate of the Classroom

Starting on the first day of class, the teacher begins to influence the development of a mood, a climate, and atmosphere that will characterize each class. This environment will have both positive and negative effects on learning, and teachers are aware of the intangible differences from one class to another. A technique or style of teaching that works beautifully in one course falls flat in the next. Students in one class will energetically direct their efforts toward learning the subject matter; those in another will be apathetic and nonresponsive. Some classes are highly supportive of the teacher; others contain students who are openly hostile and who develop sophisticated techniques for undermining discussions.

The dynamics of a class are complicated and often confusing but they cannot be ignored. Different types of students are motivated by different emotions and each type places unique pressures on the teacher. The students themselves are often in conflict between their desire to maintain individuality and the pressures to conform to what may be the contrary norms of the group. Most students are gregarious and are often sidetracked by their misperceptions of the attitudes and personalities of other members of the class. Over the course of a school term, the teacher and various clusters of students change the basis and quality of their relationship; the magnitude and direction of these changes depends significantly on the ability of the teacher to adapt his behavior to the needs of his students.

Roles Teachers Play

Different styles of teaching are often categorized as "types"—Drillmaster, Content-centered, Instructor-centered, Intellect-centered, and Person-centered (Axelrod, 1970). Different sets of labels are used depending on the aspects of teaching performances being observed. More specifically and apart from any "typing" schemes, how does a teacher answer questions? Does he listen carefully and establish eye contact with the questioner, or does he deprecate the question and refuse to answer it? Does he allow students to question and give answers to one another, or does he insist upon being part of every verbal interchange? Are there chauvinistic signals with respect to sex, youth, race, religion, educational ability and the like? How does the teacher's relationship to individuals in the class affect the mood of the entire group? Answers to questions of this kind have an important bearing on the classroom climate and may determine whether or not the teacher has the support of his students and to what extent he and his course will influence intellectual and personal change.

Richard Mann and his colleagues (1970) have reported the results of a detailed study of the verbal interaction that takes place in a college classroom. Their analytical scheme made it possible to look at a teacher's effectiveness in terms of the role he chose to emphasize or de-emphasize. Mann's typology consisted of six categories although the first two were most typical at the University of Michigan where the study was made.

The teacher as expert:
This aspect of the teacher role conjures up the disparity between teacher and student with respect to the knowledge, experience, and wisdom they can apply to the subject matter of the course. The teacher is the expert, at least within certain defined areas of knowledge. His presumed expertise underlies both his right to be there and the students' interest in taking the course. (p. 2)

The teacher as formal authority:
Viewed from the perspective of the larger social structure within which the college classroom is located, the teacher is an agent not only of instruction but also of control and evaluation. He is responsible to a group of administrators and external agents who expect him to insure uniformity of standards and a justifiable evaluation system based on merit when he presents his set of grades at the end of the course. (p. 3)

While the other four roles were less common, they were very important to many students: the teacher as socializing agent, as facilitator, as ego ideal, and as person.

The Mann group was concerned with understanding the interchanges between the teachers and students in the classes they observed. Their task was complicated by several factors. Every classroom exchange has at least two sides. A teacher may make a statement which he recognizes as fact (here he sees himself as the expert). One student may accept the statement as it is presented. Another student in the same audience may completely miss the content of the statement and retain only an affective aura, "How did he ever think of that!" To him, the teacher functions as an ego ideal. Still a third student might question the statement as fact; if the teacher rejects the challenge, the student might interpret the response as the teacher's effort to maintain control by asserting his expertise (teacher as formal authority); if not, he might see the teacher as facilitator. Analysis of a teacher's role then depends on how the student receives the teacher, and that reception differs from student to student and from class to class. The "teacher-as" typology also enables us to see whether the teacher's role is in keeping with his personality and stated classroom goals. A teacher who sees himself mainly as a subject matter expert may, without realizing it, produce a good deal of interaction in other categories. Some teachers operate frequently as socializing agents. While they see themselves as giving students critical intellectual feedback, they are in fact giving them positive reinforcement only when the students make statements that reflect the teacher's values. A teacher will often consider himself as the expert while his students accept his statements because he represents the formal authority. The dividing line between these categories is tenuous.

Students, of course, differ from one another as distinctly as do their teachers and they too can be "typed." Any set of conceptual portraits, however, that might be useful for research purposes or for analyzing the actions of a class and its subgroups would be grossly inadequate as a basis for individual counseling or tutoring. Within these limits, the Mann group showed how the personalities of teachers and students sometimes clash, but more often become mutually supportive of the educational purpose. They identified clusters of student characteristics that can serve as "types"—at least for research and descriptive purposes:

1. The compliant students—the typical "good students" in the traditional task-oriented classroom.
2. The anxious, dependent students—angry on the in-

side but mostly frightened on the outside, dependent on the teacher for knowledge and support and anxious about being evaluated.

3. The discouraged workers—tend to blame themselves and do not turn much hostility toward other people.
4. The independents—significantly bolder than other students, self-confident, and not often threatened by the teacher, their work, or other students.
5. The heroes—male only, productive and creative but at the same time hostile and resentful.
6. The snipers—with a low level of self-esteem and elusive when confronted directly with an issue.
7. The attention-seekers—predominantly social rather than intellectual in their orientation.
8. The silent students—nonparticipating and helpless and vulnerable in relation to the teacher.

By the time they reach college most students have been "socialized" to accept the definition the teacher sets for his own role in the classroom; within limits, they accept the format put forward by the teacher. If the teacher says he will lecture every class period, the students settle down into their own familiar roles of listener, note taker, perhaps occasional questioner, and test taker. The teacher is, of course, not the sole determinant but generally speaking it is his responsibility to direct the activities of the class toward the course objectives and to utilize the available resources, including the social factors within the classroom group.

In any event these personal interactions vary from class to class partly as a function of the task that defines the purpose of the group. The results of research on task-oriented groups outside the educational setting indicate some of the specific interactions that lead to productive group effort. These findings can be applied to several different instructional arrangements.

The Class as a Work Group

In his study of industrial work groups, Rensis Likert (1961) found that the pattern of within-group communication was one of the more consistent differences between the effective and the ineffective groups. Looking at the decision-making process in these work groups, Likert concluded that in the more effective groups, each member related to all the other members and to the supervisor as part of the group. The members of the work group ("subordinates" in Fig. 3) actually begin to take on some of the leadership functions of the group.

In less effective work groups, the pattern of communication generally follows what Likert refers to as the "man-to-man" pattern. Here, each subordinate works at building an exclusive relationship with his superior, for it is this relationship which he sees as having the greatest potential payoff. A group managed in this style is less productive and its members less highly motivated than a group in which horizontal communication is encouraged.

The interaction in the conventional classroom

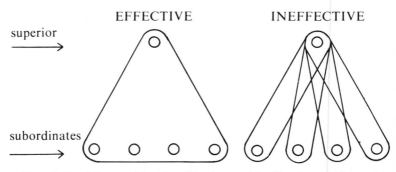

Fig. 3. Decision making in effective and ineffective work groups (Redrawn from Likert, 1961)

setting is closer to the man-to-man pattern than to the pattern characterized by high peer leadership. Establishing a classroom group with effective horizontal communication and peer leadership is difficult, particularly in a course that meets for only a few hours a week. A college course is not usually a team effort, but Likert's point is well taken—output is better when individuals within a group respond openly to one another.

The Teacher as Leader

Another way of looking at the whole question of how a teacher influences his classes is to ask about the kind of leadership he provides. The literature on leadership is extensive, but for our purposes the theory of leadership devised by David Bowers and Stanley Seashore (1969) provides an excellent framework. Their work isolates four major factors of leadership:

1. *Support:* the extent to which a supervisor shows personal consideration for his subordinates by being approachable and hearing what they say
2. *Interaction facilitation:* the extent to which a supervisor encourages his subordinates to work as a team and to share ideas and opinions
3. *Goal emphasis:* the extent to which a supervisor encourages his subordinates to work as a team and sets an example by working hard
4. *Work facilitation:* the extent to which a supervisor gives his subordinates the tools (training, ideas, help in planning) to do a more effective job

Leadership that is strong on all four factors emphasizes both task and socioemotional aspects of the job. Such a leader must set high standards for his subordinates and give them the tools to reach these standards; he must be supportive of them as people and at the same time help them to build their own channels of support and communication. Flanders (1960) observed that a teacher must strike a balance between dependence and independence in the classroom. Balanced leadership of this kind may be difficult to provide within the time pressures of a semester. Research findings from both industry and education suggest that more time than is now the case needs to be devoted to developing good communication and leadership within the classroom group.

Classroom Dynamics—Summary

Discussions of effective teaching generally concentrate on the intellectual task and tend to neglect the accompanying, often disabling, aspects of the group's emotional state, of the frustrations, anxieties, and aspirations. Teachers who approach their students with intellectual superiority do so often out of a distorted impression of how the teacher-as-expert relates to students-as-learners. The teacher who scorns students often creates a climate which encourages hostile students to challenge him and insecure students to accept his scorn and to look for failure. The pressure students apply in such a situation may provoke the troubled teacher to precipitously abdicate his role as expert in a panicked effort to relieve tension. Both teacher and student under these circumstances reach a stalemate, a "holding of the breath" until the semester's end. The emotional climate has seriously deterred the learning process.

Similarly the issue of power and authority is always present in the classroom, no matter how sincerely a teacher seeks to allay his students' fears at the beginning of each semester. The reality of any classroom is distorted when a teacher presents himself as the authority and simultaneously chides his students for their anxiety over grades or other authority issues. The teacher who seeks to avoid being viewed as an authority and yet has a compelling need to maintain control of his class generates emotional reactions in his students that are detrimental to learning. On the other hand, the teacher who establishes that he does indeed hold real power has taken the first step toward making it possible to share that power with his students. He can do so by encouraging their participation in decisions relating to deadlines, exam format, topics of discussion, and so forth. The issue of power and authority need no longer dominate the relationship between teacher and student.

Instructional Arrangements

The lecture, the discussion group, the laboratory, the clinic or field study, and tutorial or independent study, in various combinations are the usual modes of instruction available to a teacher. The "best" arrangement, of course, depends on what is to be learned and all the conditions relating thereto. After reviewing the available literature on methods of college teaching, Dubin and Taveggia in *The Teaching-Learning Paradox* (1968) concluded that methods of teaching had little effect on significant differences in subject-matter achievement as measured by content examinations, admittedly a narrow measure of instructional impact. Frank Costin (1972) made a similar critical review:

> All in all, research has failed to disclose consistent differences in the extent to which students gain knowledge from lectures, as compared with the knowledge they obtain under such methods as discussion, projects, reading, self-study, or laboratory

work. . . . In general, however, the economy of teaching by lecture does not seem to be gained at the expense of acquiring knowledge. On the other hand, when it comes to developing skills in manipulating knowledge, as in interpreting information and solving problems, the evidence points to discussion, and possibly projects, as having an advantage over lecturing. (p. 22)

Costin pointed out that *research-based* answers to the question: "Does it really make any difference as to the method we use in our teaching, insofar as student achievement is concerned?" require specific attention to such factors as: criteria of course outcomes; teaching style; students' attitudes, and statistical versus practical significance.

A given class may be the educational coalescence that some few students have been waiting for: the right combination of content and teaching to bring educational aspirations into focus. The research findings, however, have not led to techniques for "matching up" a particular student with a particular kind of teacher or class group. Fortunately, most college students can make these decisions themselves, given the relevant information, e.g., is this a student-centered or a teacher-centered course; "square" or "open"; large in size or small? By itself, class size is a nonissue but it does carry with it certain conditions with respect to classroom climate.

Class Size

For the past forty-five years investigators have tried to find quantitative answers to the class-size question—usually by comparing the score on subject-matter examinations made by students in large versus small classes. In terms of how much and how well the students learn, few significant differences have been found. By itself, this conclusion would indicate that a department might favorably consider combining two or more small classes into one larger course. Many teachers resist such actions since, to them, the question of class size really means how many students can I teach in one class and still retain some degree of interchange and recognize each student as an individual person? Wilbert McKeachie (1971) has concluded on the basis of his own quarter-century of research and his survey of the literature, that:

> . . . The results favor student-centered teaching for the more complex educational outcomes.
>
> These results are so consistent that they suggest a greater effort should be made to train teachers in the skills of student-centered discussion teaching. A student-centered discussion is not simply one in which the instructor abdicates and sits in the back of the classroom. Failures with student-centered teaching often come when teachers find that skills of listening, democratic decision making, conflict resolution, etc., are not in their repertoire. Moreover, students need to learn new skills in order to make optimal use of a student-centered classroom. The teacher needs to know how to help students learn these skills as well as the course content. These skills can be learned, and some success in using them will, in turn, reinforce the underlying attitudes toward students and learning basic to student-centered teaching. . . ."
> (p. 3)

In addition to being expensive in terms of teacher/student ratios, small classes are more difficult to teach—if full advantage is taken of the dynamics within these smaller groups. Class size is a convenient and measurable condition but a "pure" class-size experiment would be quite uninspired if not ludicrous, e.g., does the size of the class make any dif-

ference to the viewers of an instructional film? A
more practical approach is to study resources related
to class size: given large classes, what is the best use
that can be made of teaching assistants, of the library,
of the computer and other technological aids, and of
tutoring help from undergraduate students, of different methods and frequency of testing; and can student participation be increased by adapting various
methods for group discussion? In other words, given
the reality of large classes, what is the most effective
use that can be made of the available resources?
In essence:

1. Small classes are desirable when:
   a) The student is expected to acquire discussion
      skills, laboratory technique, or other forms of
      learning which require close review by the in-
      structor;
   b) The student is expected to take an active part in
      the conduct of the course, i.e., providing ex-
      amples, distilling principles from discussions,
      giving reports, expressing value judgments, and
      drawing implications from the subject matter.
2. Large classes are just as effective as small classes
   for teaching well-defined factual and conceptual
   information.
3. Class-size decisions should be governed by the
   lecturing skill of the teacher, costs in time and
   money, access to supporting technological aids,
   and by the constraints imposed by the physical
   plant.

The Lecture

In the Golden Age of teaching—before printing, elec-
tricity, and grade point averages—the role of the
teacher was to conserve and transmit knowledge and
to inspire students to inquire into themselves and

into the world around them. This was done by engaging students in dialogue or by interpreting the written word. The lecture, which took its name for the religious teacher of the Middle Ages, the *Lektor*, remains the chief interface between teachers and students.

The lecture is for a majority of professors a security blanket, without which they would neither feel like teachers nor be recognized by the students as such. There are times when the lecture is the single most effective method of arousing interest and conveying information to a group of students. When certain material is not readily available or requires frequent updating, a lecturer can explore those points which he feels are pertinent. He can synthesize large bodies of material that threaten to overwhelm his students, and provide a framework within which they can organize their learning. The lecturer holds center stage and what he has to say and the way he says it dominates the interaction. Inevitably, the lecturer is a model, not only of style but of attitudes and values, biases, and beliefs. Whether or not this model is accepted by the students is of course another question.

Studies on college-level learning indicate that when lectures are arranged around questions which pique students' interest, that is, about what is *not* known rather than around mere recitations of fact, learning is improved and interest in further learning about a topic is increased (Berlyne, 1960). In particular, questions which arouse students' curiosity about novel aspects of things already familiar to them may have significant influence on the development of curiosity. Lectures which pose problems are likely to be more effective than those which present neatly encapsulated principles and facts. Such tactics draw students actively into the substance of the lecture, and research clearly shows that they learn better when they participate in the learning process than when they passively accept the output of a "distant" speaker. Variations have been tried toward improving the instructional impact of the straight lecture, but results are not especially impressive.

Seminars and Discussion Groups

The experience of participating in a seminar or small discussion group or their equivalent is absolutely basic to a good college education. Given both support and resistance from his peers, each student examines information and assesses its worth. The discussion group is an educational "testing ground" for the interchange of information, expression of attitudes, clarification of inferences, and formation of new values. As independent study and self-instruction facilities become more generally used, the discussion group will be an even more necessary resource for teaching. McKeachie (1965) has described the discussion group as being particularly appropriate when the instructor wants:

1. To give students opportunities to formulate principles in their own words and to suggest applications of these principles;
2. To help students become aware of and to define problems based on information derived from readings or lectures;
3. To gain acceptance for information or theories counter to folklore or previous beliefs of students;
4. To get feedback on how well his instructional objectives are being attained.

The composition of the group can be a significant factor in determining how well any one or all of these goals can be met. "Homogeneous" grouping in terms of academic aptitude and subject-matter proficiency is not particularly relevant but "sectioning" students along lines of student interests and motives should facilitate group interaction.

Students are relative strangers on the first day of class and it can be difficult to get a discussion started, and then keep it going. McKeachie suggests that a common error in discussion is to ask questions which obviously have only one right answer—which the instructor already knows. "How does the idea that . . . apply to . . . ?" is more likely to stimulate discussion than the question "What principle was illustrated here?" Some teachers skillfully play the role of devil's advocate as a means of stimulating discussion. Nevertheless, the wise instructor keeps in mind that participation is not an end in itself, but only the means to achieve educational objectives; he learns to appraise a group's progress and avoids letting it become a freewheeling bull session.

A good discussion leader will note the usual barriers and points of resistance within the group. He is sensitive to cues indicating inattention, hostility, or diversionary tactics. Conflicts generally arise in an active discussion, and a skilled leader can utilize these as a contribution toward learning; if left ambiguous and uncertain, they may cause continuing trouble. Thus, at every meeting the teacher is involved with the dynamics of the group. He meets apathy, indifference, anxiety, and hostility, but also curiosity, enthusiasm, affection, excitement, ambition, and cooperation. These are the attitudes that impede or accelerate learning; they come close to the surface in the discussion group, and they are intimately linked to the intellectual content of the course. A discussion group succeeds when students can actively test their ideas in this forum of their peers.

The Laboratory

The primary interaction in the instructional laboratory is between the individual student as a simulated scientist and selected aspects of a science. The laboratory instructor and the other students are simply there, sometimes as distractors, as general facilitators, or as a source of help with technical procedures. The instructional laboratory is a cognitive exercise in the acquisition of knowledge about research methodology. The student learns how to define a problem and plan an experiment, gains technical skill in setting up equipment and procedures, acquires accuracy in observing the experimental effect, and derives logical inferences and generalizations from the data. In the laboratory, the abstractions of a domain of knowledge take a significant step toward concrete reality and this can be exciting. Without constant attention, however, laboratory exercises can regress to a mechanical operation where the aim of the "experiment" is to fill in the blanks in the lab manual.

A recent development in laboratory teaching is the use of computers to simulate experimental conditions and to simulate the design of different data-gathering procedures for hypothesis testing. Students become involved in the analysis of good-versus-poor research plans rather than spending most of their time with the routine mechanics of a single project. Dana Main and Sabin Head (1971) report, ". . . a small *scientific community* was created with discussions and problem-solving experiences that were not possible before" (p. 427). Improving the impact of the undergraduate instructional laboratory is the major challenge to the science departments if they would protect this high-cost mode of teaching.

Instruction in the Field

Off-campus resources are being used more widely, and in a number of cities "experimental" high schools have been established for the express purpose of making better use of community resources for all the students—the college bound as well as for those traditionally tagged for "vocational training." At the university level the medical internship, the social work field placement and "practice teaching" used to stand quite alone; they are now joined by field work in clinical psychology, clinical law, clinical sociology, as well as in economics, political science, and other disciplines. Students learn a great deal from the real world extensions of lecture, laboratory, and textbook knowledge, but this involvement often brings complications—confusion and frustration from feeling unable to participate in a meaningful way with concrete problems. Nevertheless, the in-depth experience of observing, working, and learning within the environment of a mental hospital, for example, has no substitute in the text, in the film, in simulation, or in a case-book treatise. Field study puts students at one point of the interchange between their discipline and the needs of society, e.g., chemistry and drugs, physics and energy resources, biology and environment, psychology and mental health, economics and inflation, political science and the voter's franchise, geology and natural resources, sociology and population, education and the handicapped child. The teacher of almost any "outreach" type course must be prepared to meet counter proposals from his students as they redefine issues of "relevance."

Tutorial Instruction

The Socratic dialogue was a tutorial technique and this form of instruction weaves in and out and through the history of higher education. Individual instruction is as important today as it ever was, but it is becoming increasingly difficult to bring about. The press of student numbers and the high costs of education tend to relegate individual instruction to the academic archives for retrieval at some indefinite future. Only the respect of teachers for students as individuals, and the high regard of students for one another can prevent this from happening.

Tutoring was revived in the early 1960s as college students became involved with educationally deprived children in Civil Rights activities in the South. It was soon realized that similar needs existed in northern communities, and by 1965 over 100,000 college students were active in some 350 full-fledged tutorial projects (Hamilton, 1965). These tutors were the "haves" helping the "have nots" and with the missionary zeal of a new educational charity. Tutoring of this type has a quite different meaning from the revered traditions of "Oxbridge"; it is a low-cost educational resource with two-way benefits for both tutor and taught and not, necessarily, in a remedial situation.

The self-paced supervised study arrangements described in Chapter 7 frequently involve undergraduates as assistant teachers and as tutors in a one-to-one situation or with a small group of other students. This is a far more constructive use of a tutor than as a last resort toward passing a course. The two-student dyad has been further developed by Marcel Goldschmid (1971) in "the learning cell" as an excellent instructional resource. In effect, two students take turns as tutor and the tutored while proceeding through a unit previously studied or through new material. Most teachers will affirm that there is no better way to learn than to teach, and this advantage is supported by all the research on the learning effects of active participation.

Independent Study

As a generic concept, independent study is an instrument for individual instruction on campus or off. As Paul Dressel and Mary Thompson (1973) report, it takes many forms but its most valued purpose is to replace passive dependence on a teacher with independent inquiry; to put things together in one's own way; to select and carry through with a topic that is worthwhile and interesting. The student enrolled in course "Independent Study 499" is already doing what many of the instructional support procedures seek to bring about in the conventional classroom; to learn how to learn independently. In its best form, independent reading, review, and recitation allow the student to gather together the information necessary to further his academic progress. He learns how dependent one must be on the contributions of others when forming information into a different pattern. Insofar as teachers can help, fine, but we should not underestimate the ability of individual students to go it alone when the goal seems worthwhile. The support of the teacher is important and should be available when asked for. Guidance during the early stages helps to reduce trial-and-error searching among irrelevant references, to limit the independent study objectives to something less than scientific breakthroughs, ultimate social-policy position papers, or the definitive work of criticism.

The lowest form of independent study is to

"give" students a period of "free" time prior to the taking of a required comprehensive examination. This is instructional exploitation; forcing a student into a pre-established faculty mold under the guise of freedom and independence. Independent learning requires that the student demonstrate to himself that he can select and utilize pertinent knowledge for solving a problem or to make a point. To this extent, he is achieving directly what teachers try to bring about in the more involved procedures of classroom instruction.

This chapter has offered a general discussion of the interaction between teacher and student, and has then considered the application of interaction effects in the different modes of teaching. From the two-person tutorial on up, every class is a socially interacting group. The effective management of the dynamics of the group, taking into account student expectation and subject-matter limitations, is a prime dimension of good teaching. The process of learning is personal, private, and unique with each student, but social factors in his classes, on campus, and in the community have a powerful influence on what he learns and how well. The hyphenated phrase, teaching-learning, is shorthand for indicating that one of the most important functions of the teacher is to organize and manage these social-group factors in support of the learning process.

In his recent book *Alternatives to the Traditional* (1972), Ohmer Milton describes the many different forms of college instruction today. Whatever the specifications might be for a particular instructional arrangement, the discriminating teacher will carefully appraise the extent to which these new procedures support the conditions for learning—including the social factors to which students (and teachers) are so responsive.

Person to person interactions are most conspicuous in tutoring and in discussion groups but they also determine the climate for learning in the lecture, the clinic, and infield studies. The book, the film, audio and video cassettes, and the computer are aids for the personal processing of information, but solo learning is only a "study break" between social interchanges with other persons. One of the more conspicuous mistakes in putting together an automated study system is to overlook the basic need of students to organize their thoughts, feelings, and beliefs via the interaction with other persons.

Chapter 11

Technology and Instruction

The treasure hunt continues for the technological device that can clear the air, cure the ill, trim the belly, enhance the ego, and educate the young. Already, education is a mammoth user of technology and as the budget squeeze gets tighter, more will be heard about using technology as a cost-saving measure in teaching. In counteraction, questions will be raised as to what is happening to the quality of education and to the personal influence of the teacher and the personal development of the student.

Loosely defined, "technology" refers both to devices such as cassettes and procedures such as simulation; in practice, most attention is given to mechanical and electronic equipment. This fixation on "hardware" tends to overlook the fact that the book is the most widely used "technological" aid, and the library has, for a long time, been the technological center of the university. In comparison, the television center, the audio-visual center, the testing center, the media resources center, the copy center, and now the computing center, are subsidiaries recently added. Teachers turn to these media units for assistance in bringing particular sources of information to their classes: to extend or supplement the lecture and the textbook.

In an effort to reduce instructional costs, many schools have used technology as an out-and-out substitute for the teacher. There are occasions when budget and other restraints make a live teacher unavailable, and automated teaching is certainly better than no presentation at all. The fact that a course can now be given to distant and unseen classes is an important advantage to many students who might otherwise be left out. But how to make information available is a different question from how to improve the quality of teaching. Furthermore, technological teaching systems, while extending availability, have not turned out to be a money-saving measure because the "machines" themselves require a continually expanding support system:

> . . . the new informational technology will eventually reduce instructional costs below levels possible using conventional methods alone, but, in the short run, it will only increase costs. It will be financially prudent to concentrate early investments in areas with the greatest capability for wide use: (a) libraries, (b) adult education, (c) primary and secondary education, and (d) introductory courses in higher education where basic skills are involved, like mathematics and language. (Carnegie Commission on Higher Education, 1972, p. 3)

With expanded use, technology may become a cost benefit factor in education; in the meantime, the teacher's concern is to use these aids to improve the impact of his here-and-now course. The manufacturers of instructional equipment arrange impressive convention-booth displays and write exciting promotional literature, but they are trying to sell something rather than to teach something. The experienced teacher is wary of "advantages" offered by media men for devices that were invented elsewhere, that is, outside education. Little is gained, for example, by changing the medium of stimulus presentation—from seeing and hearing to hearing alone; from reading to viewing, from hearing to seeing, and so on. Generally speaking, such changes in the input channel have insignificant effects on learning. Far more important is the use of technology to enable the teacher to strengthen course content and to permit each student to learn at the rate, and in a manner, that best fits his individual capabilities.

The Visual Image

At one time the maximum size for a lecture course was determined by how far back a student could sit and still read the writing on the blackboard. Today a professor can extend his words and drawings farther than his own eye can see. The use of visual-image technology to "broadcast" information, however, is secondary to the tremendous increase in the variety and quality of visual materials becoming available as a *resource for learning*.

Television

Television, live and on tape, is the device most often seen as the efficient solution for the problem of how to teach greater numbers of students—a teacher can be rolled up in the can and "distributed" to any number of classrooms. More specifically, with television, a lecture demonstration can be magnified; objects can be examined in slow motion, stop action, at high speeds, and even stroboscopically. Television can observe in places where direct observation is dangerous (in a radiation laboratory) or distracting (in a clinical interview) or not feasible (in an operating room); it can bring remote events into the classroom. The advent of relatively inexpensive and sturdy portable video-tape recorders (VTR) has given the teacher much more flexibility in selecting, preparing, and organizing curricular materials for visual presentation. With a camera, a television tape recorder, and monitors, the teacher can make and display his own tapes with a minimum of effort and time. VTR has many of the capabilities of live instructional television and few of its drawbacks. The tape can be played back immediately on any number of television screens and can be transferred to 16-mm film or 8-mm film, on a reel or in a cassette. Whatever can be televised can also be recorded on video tape, simply and economically, and those tapes can be erased and reused when the recorded information is no longer needed.

Instructors can use VTR as an erasable blackboard on which to try, test, and immediately criticize visual aids. Demonstrations can be filmed and erased if they appear inappropriate. Students can prepare tapes of their work which can be criticized by the professor. By watching themselves on video tape, student teachers and graduate teaching assistants (as well as professors) can evaluate their own classroom techniques. Colloquia can be video taped and distributed to neighboring schools, making the resources of a large university available, at little expense, to small colleges. VTR is, however, a relatively expensive medium for information storage; its most economical use is for presenting visual information of short-lived importance.

Films and Cassettes

Film is a familiar medium to most teachers. It is more costly to produce than video tapes and is used to fullest advantage when recording phenomena of lasting value. In those instances where the visual image is itself the subject of detail study, "high fidelity" projection is, of course, a necessary condition. Otherwise, teacher-made films can have as much instructional value as those made professionally. Novel, colorful, magnified, or moving images may not by themselves make it easier for a student to understand a concept unless these images are intrinsically relevant to the subject under study. The development of the single concept 8-mm cartridge units has made the film a more flexible medium for learning. The film loop antedates the video tape cassette but in function, they are the same.

The cassette can be used in the laboratory or at home, in a classroom or auditorium, in a dormitory or library. It enables an instructor to clarify an idea, teach a skill, repeat an operation, pose a problem, or provide one or many illustrations of a theme. The instructor can, if he has access to a movie or television camera, make his own films or tapes for his own classes, and he can dub in his own commentary. Because they repeat endlessly, cassette loops can carry information of high density, enabling students to "peel off" layers of material in successive viewings. Stop action and frame-by-frame advance allow close study; the student can view and review the film (or video cassette) until he attains a satisfactory level of meaning and understanding. Students control the cassette in the same way that they control a record player, tape recorder, or the pace of reading a book. The individual use of the visual image as a resource for independent study is a dramatic step forward from the original employment of television as an instrument for mass teaching.

The Still Picture

The still visual image is adequate for most instructional purposes. The overhead projector, for example, allows the instructor to put a drawing on a screen and to guide his class through its intricacies. The development of the sound-on-slide combination allows the teacher to prepare self-contained units of instruction (modules) that can be used by students off campus or in independent study programs. If motion is extraneous to the instructional point, the considerable extra cost of film or VTR over slides, film strips, and the overhead projector is an extravagance. A spontaneously drawn schematic diagram on the blackboard is hard to beat as an aid for clarifying technical detail or an abstract principle.

Hearing Things

Teachers do a lot of talking, and talking can easily be recorded. Audio technology is relatively inexpensive and a dial-access system, for example, allows students to dial-a-lecture and to hear the inflections, the points of emphasis, and other subtle expressions that interlace the substantive treatment itself. A sound source, however, does not hold attention as well as does the visual image, especially when the sound waves are not responded to directly as in music, but require cognitive translation as in listening to a lecture. There are instances where the *necessary* element for learning is carried by audio cues. A medical student cannot learn to discriminate heart sounds or chest sounds by reading or by watching oscilloscope tracings alone. Poetry listening adds something to poetry reading. Drama heard is usually better than drama read. The listening room in the campus library is a popular and educationally worthwhile site for learning.

Ideally, each student should have independent control over the start, stop, and repetitions of the instructional tape, as in the language laboratory. Otherwise, he is simply one in a class listening to a centrally controlled sequence of audio information. A less costly alternative, for purposes of listening, is the portable tape recorder which enables the student to take his "carrel" with him and set it up almost anywhere—in his room, at the park, or in the car (as commuters frequently do). The student can listen to or review a prerecorded lecture as his "homework" assignment.

The Computer as an Aid for Learning

The report by the Carnegie Commission on Higher Education on the uses of technology was titled *The Fourth Revolution* (1972). This title was taken from an earlier publication by Eric Ashby (1967), who marked the first revolution when the task of educating the young was shifted from parents to teachers, from the home to the school. Using the *written* word to convey information was the next important change, and the invention of printing led to the third revolution. "The fourth revolution . . . is portended by developments in electronics, notably those involving the radio, television, tape recorder, and computer" (p. 9). Of these, computer technology is the most powerful and was represented in greater detail as dominating the "Fourth Revolution." It is indeed an exciting technology for education which will, in time, give the student a flexible tool for learning; it will change the nature of instruction, the boundaries of the campus, and the role of both teachers and students.

These are still the early days in the educational applications of computer technology. The heavy costs of computer hardware, and equally expensive software demands, have prevented the widespread use of this medium. Based on an analytical survey of knowledgeable practitioners, Ernest Anastasio and Judith Morgan (1972) have categorized the major factors inhibiting the use of computers in instruction:

1. Production and distribution of instructional materials
2. Demonstration of the effectiveness of CAI (Computer Assisted Instruction)
3. Theory of instruction (need for additional psychological and educational research)
4. Educational system and the teacher (the general resistance to change)
5. Cost
6. Technical research and development

These factors cannot be ranked in order of importance; some are general, others specific, and their inhibiting effects will vary in degree from one school to another.

Local Applications

Computer-based instructional programs cannot be purchased at the local bookstore or ordered from a central supplier, plugged in, and turned over to students. CAI is not, at best, a mass teaching procedure and the capability of the computer is underused if the same material is presented, in the same sequence, to each student. Why use a $1 million computer to replace, in function, a $10 book? This has been a common mistake, probably because programmed learning, the teaching machine, and CAI were "invented" in overlapping sequence. It was thought that prompt feedback to a student's response, as in the first two, would be the essential factor, and the early applications of CAI used linear, frame-by-frame programming as the basic model. From this relatively primitive beginning, computer applications have expanded along several different lines.

1. *Drill and practice.* The computer is used as a tutor giving questions to the student and then confirming or correcting the response, or guiding the student toward making a reply which can then be evaluated. The material being "taught" is information that students should acquire for its own value or as prerequisite for later course work. Language learning is a good example. In one project (Wood, 1972) an entire series of drills and exercises on German grammar are programmed for computer presentation. The computer terminal points out errors made by the student, and with the flexibility of the computer the student is able to move backwards to previous drills at any time, to look at his past performance records, to consult an English-German dictionary, to skip later exercises in each drill, or, if his performance warrants, to play German games.

2. *Simulation and gaming.* These technologies, described in Chapter 9, are especially well suited to computer control. The computer can be programmed to simulate a prototype scientific experiment, a hospital patient, a student meeting with his counselor, or a reference librarian interacting with a student. In social and political science games the student can play the role of policy maker, faced with the same kinds of uncertainties and conflicting goals that confront the actual policy maker in the real world. Whether the computer is playing chess or simulating the national economy, a business enterprise, or an ecological system, the student enters his decision into the computer and receives the consequences of his action. A

series of decisions may be called for in reaching an optimal solution to an assigned problem and at any point the student may need to take corrective action before moving ahead. Thus, more important than the giving of information (which books and manuals can do) is the role of the computer in interacting with intellective decision making by students as shown by the following two examples in the use of the computer:

a) Students in an undergraduate course in experimental psychology use computer-based exercises to simulate various research designs. By holding the values of certain variables constant and by systematically altering the values of one or more other variables, they can test different hypotheses. They gain experience in following research programs which would have been possible only at considerable cost of time, effort, and the facilities of a real laboratory (Rajecki, 1972).

b) Undergraduates in macroeconomic policy courses use this technology for learning how economic policies are developed and altered via a computer simulation of a world economy composed of ten essentially equivalent countries. In each country consumers and business firms are assumed to regulate their spending according to income, prices, interest rates, and so forth, while the policy maker has control of taxes, government spending, and money supply. Each group is to achieve the best possible degree of full employment, price stability, economic growth, and balance of payment equilibrium. Students are provided with necessary data and their decisions are fed into the computer which solves for new values of all relevant variables (Holbrook, 1972).

3. *Model building and problem solving.* As a lightning-fast slide rule and sketch pad, the computer generates rapid feedback on the decisions relative to

problem solving, curve fitting, model building, rule discovery, application of principles, and many other cognitive functions that are difficult for the student to "practice" in the laboratory, the clinic, the classroom, or in the natural setting. A student can manipulate parameters in computer-generated visual displays, designs, and models where his attention is focused on the underlying principle or the rules reflected in a sequence of specific instances. For example, a camera can be attached to a cathode-ray tube computer terminal and from this arrangement a series of animated instructional films can be produced. These films enable introductory students in astronomy to visualize orbital motions of planets around the sun and other space/time relations of the astronomical system (Teske, 1972).

The educational value of a computer-based problem-solving program lies in the opportunity it gives a student to derive generalizations and rules, and to carry these through to the applied setting. Although data processing may be involved, the computer is also being used as a "logic" machine. The teacher faces a challenging task—to program the computer to teach "good judgment" on the part of his problem-solving students.

4. *Information retrieval*. The user at a computer terminal can gain access to extensive "files" of bibliographic (library) information which might not otherwise be available except at considerable expense of time and travel. The chronic problem, however, is how to index information for retrieval; by what means can key terms be identified and agreed upon as "entry" words for certain kinds of information? A partial solution is to use the almost unlimited cross-indexing capability of a computer storage system. The student can select the index terms for searching,

and these key words will call up references pertaining to his interests since these references were originally indexed under several headings.

5. *Educational computer networks.* This category might include any or all of the preceding functions but in the initial phase of network development greater attention has been given to the more conventional data-processing functions. In principle, however, whatever advantages the computer holds for local educational use applies to network operations. The computer has the potential for serving teachers and students geographically separated from one another, or from a central store of knowledge and information. Computer terminals can be dispensed as are telephone sets, and the spatial separation of terminals from the central computer is, except for line charges, irrelevant. Concerted effort, however, is required to overcome obstacles on three fronts: administration of such a network, the system engineering problems, and the development of educationally valid materials for network delivery.

An excellent example of a computer network designed to serve educational purposes is the Michigan Educational Research and Information Triad (MERIT) that links the separate computer systems at Michigan State University, Wayne State University, and the University of Michigan. In time, it is expected that the MERIT network will extend to schools throughout the state, and to computer systems beyond state boundaries. Teachers and students at remote terminals will have access to a tremendous computer system to support their local computer needs. Significant steps have been taken to access basic files of information. *Chemical Titles,* for example, is a biweekly, computer-readable journal that reports the titles of selected papers recently pub-

lished in approximately 650 current chemical journals. Although direct instructional use of the network
system by students lies down the road a way, the
implications for the future are impressive.

Supporting Services for the Teacher

Subject-matter teachers do not need to be particularly knowledgeable about how computers work, but
they will usually benefit from consultation with specialists in an educational service and research facility
as to what the local computer can and cannot do. The
working out of the specific features of a computer-
based teaching plan will be speeded and supported
by:

1. *The clearinghouse function.* Most current reports are in the form of preprints, conference reports,
technical papers, and personal communications
which circulate within a rather limited network of
fellow investigators. From one to three years later
many of these items may appear in book form as part
of an anthology on the state of the art. A few journals
report studies and opinion pieces about educational
technology but these are usually heavily laden with
the jargon of the trade, since they are aimed at professional and technical specialists rather than at the
subject-matter teacher. The broader treatment cuts
across discipline lines and so omits the detail needed
by a teacher seeking information about how to prepare a computer-based program for a specific unit of
knowledge. Considerable time and effort will be
saved if a teacher has access to a facility where he
can read reports and talk with specialists about current trends, new developments, and who is doing
what computer work pertinent to his own projected
plans.

2. *Author training and consultation.* In the CAI

world, the term "author" designates the subject-matter specialist responsible for mapping out the computer-based unit. The "programmer" then codes this information into the language selected (probably by another specialist) as being most appropriate for storing and managing the instructional material. The time required to "author" a 30- to 50-minute instructional program is substantial and is the type of skill for which a workshop or short training program is helpful. The do-it-yourself author is prone to the common fault of underusing the capabilities of the computer.

Technical assistance is usually needed for selecting a computer language from a growing inventory of programming languages. "A comparative study of programming languages listed over 40 different languages and dialects which have been developed especially for instructional use of computers . . ." (K. Zinn, 1971). Consultation with a language specialist will save the author considerable time frustration, and perhaps out-and-out failure. A computer is not all things to all people, and each local "system" can perform certain functions better than others. The teacher-author will need to know which languages are available, how charges are determined, what special input-output capabilities are needed, such as graphic display, what demand will be made on the memory store, and other conditions which may be required to comply with the local computer system.

The student is not a stable, fixed, and uniform component of the CAI system. He is a variable quantity with a qualitative style and his own strategies for learning. For example, the return "wrong" from the computer may be all the information that is necessary for some students while others anxiously wait for specific and detailed instructions as to "what do I do now?" This variable needs to be considered. In other instances the teacher may need technical help for integrating noncomputer components, e.g., slides, films, and tapes into his instructional unit. Several revisions are usually necessary to ensure the quality of a program but pride of authorship may weaken critical self-examination as to what changes should be made. Design and evaluation specialists are frequently helpful in this review and refereeing function.

3. *Research support for instructional development.* The list of supporting services can be long or short, but the grisly matter of money hangs over the entire scene of computer usage for instruction. Prototype programs are especially expensive in teacher time, computer time, technician time, and consultation time. This large outlay is followed by another wave of expenses to phase the CAI units into normal instructional use. In most instances, therefore, instructional programming should be considered in the context of a research and development program. For college-level subject matter, the teacher must be involved to select and to assess the organization of the content material and to integrate the computer-based unit with the other resources available to his students. Other specialists contribute information about the technical requirements of the computer system, such as "software" (language) options which may be most appropriate for programming a particular instructional unit, or about the human factors represented by the students working at the computer terminals. Team expertise gives some assurance that the computer-based instructional unit will be in a form students can manage and find worth their effort. Many CAI projects end up in a pedagogical blind alley and for the same reasons that most instructional

innovations fail to take root and survive: they turn out to be educationally trivial or are too demanding of the teacher's time, are boring and dreary to students, are too expensive, or continue to be plagued by procedural "bugs." These are some of the reasons most of the successful instructional computer applications are closely tied to a research and development group.

Long-Range Issues

The teacher, the student, and the book compose an educational troika that works and is, understandably, resistant to change. Education tends to be conservative because teachers have often found that highly touted innovations from off-campus sources rarely turn out to make much difference in how well students learn. Any technological replacement for the book, such as the computer, must demonstrate that it can do a better job of serving the information processing requirements of the student. The teacher is usually in the best position to make the first judgment and, since technology is becoming less costly and adapted to decentralized use, it is more often being judged by the faculty as compatible with their individual teaching responsibilities.

During the past ten years a group of educational research specialists and administrators in the Big Ten universities have compiled an annual abstract *Development and Experiment in College Teaching* which reports successful on-going or completed instructional projects at the participating institutions. An analysis of the contents of these reports (S. C. Ericksen, 1973) showed that of the 279 abstracts, about one-third referenced the use of one or more technological aids—computers, visual and audio devices, and multimedia arrangements. Projects of this nature were reported by almost every major unit within these schools and one must conclude that teachers will more and more become involved in the development and use instructional technology.

Faculty Involvement

To repeat a frequent refrain in this book, m.ost affairs in teaching revolve about three basic responsibilities: (1) content decisions as to what students should learn, (2) classroom management, and (3) evaluation of student achievement. Good teaching requires coherence and consistency among these aspects of instruction, and the use of technological media does not alter this basic paradigm. Faculty members tend to give first priority to content, since students are without redress if what they learn via any medium is outdated, irrelevant, or incorrect. Teachers contribute to the substance of what should be learned through the medium of the printed word—reference books, textbooks, and syllabi. The successful use of the newer technologies requires that this effort be expanded to include the production of instructional material for slides, films, video tapes, computer programs, and the like.

The insatiable appetite of technological aids for worthwhile content material cannot usually be satisfied by purchases from commercial sources. Exchanging teacher-produced instructional units from one school to another is a potential means of increasing supply, but requires a not yet existing information network about nonprint teaching materials and their instructional value. So far, however, authoring of media-based instructional materials by the faculty has been limited, even meager. Not having ready access to production facilities is one reason, but more pervasive is the belief that professional reputations are more quickly and firmly established through scholarly and scientific publications. Teachers quite justifiably feel that they cannot afford the time and energy needed to produce media units and to make intelligent use of technological devices in their classrooms until academia responds to these efforts with the same promotions, salary increases, and esteem that go to the researcher.

Automation can place a vast world of knowledge quite literally at the fingertips of the student. Direction from the teacher is imperative if students are to select, to evaluate, and to use this information as a base for making value judgments as to what knowledge is worth learning. The job is a demanding one and the teacher must not default the educational uses of technology by leaving this resource to those less able to define the content specifications for a given course of study.

Student Involvement

Students judge technology in terms of its usefulness for their own learning. They discount a classroom presentation which comes on as an "ersatz" teacher, or as an "enriching learning experience." Unfortunately, many students come to the campus waterlogged by excessive exposure to films as "rainy day" substitutes for an active classroom involvement. On the other hand, they will usually respond favorably to a film, a video tape, a recording, or a computer program which they perceive as being really relevant to a principle, or adding clarification to a problem.

The instructional technologies can transform education into a far more personal experience than it has ever been; fitting it to the needs and abilities of each individual student. Putting technological devices to work in this manner can be compared to the way a book is "used." A student studies a book at his own rate, he riffles the pages back and forth; he moves in and out of the book to other reference material; he tests himself; he speculates and wonders; and he leaves the book to converse with the fellow student and to range widely across discipline boundaries. The point is, *the student is in control;* he determines the sequence of information, and the rate and the frequency with which it is reviewed and evaluated.

In a well-designed, automated study carrel, the student is still in control. He can do those things that he normally does at a study desk—read a book, browse, write a paper, or solve problems. In addition he can sample and select from a variety of media materials; and for intensive learning, as mentioned earlier in connection with cassettes, he can slow down, repeat, or stop the tape, slides, film, or computer program according to his own informational needs and ability to learn. This is the way he studies a book, and this is the way, therefore, that technology can be put to work to enhance the difference between active learning and passive reading, listening, or viewing. While technology provides the student with additional sources of information, it is rarely sufficient by itself. It must nearly always include the opportunity for him to meet with his peers, and with his teacher, to engage in dialogue about implications and inferences, to test his attitudes and quality of understanding, to debate value judgments and the action implied thereby.

Institutional Involvement

Some type of media resource facility would seem to be a necessary condition for local development of technological aids for instruction. Further, the faculty should have easy access to the expertise and the equipment and, over time, this access should extend to students who may find a particular medium (other than print) especially appropriate to carrying out or reporting a specific project. On many campuses the library is becoming a multimedia resource facility, but this may not meet the campus needs with respect to the production of instructional materials. Teachers who develop these materials need strong institutional support in several forms: released time from other duties; some system of copyright protection and payment of royalties; recognition within the department, college, and institution; funds for experimentation; consulting services for technical problems and instructional design; and bibliographic recognition of the production of nonprint instructional materials.

A number of serious questions require attention from the institution as it exercises its responsibility for the educational applications of technology: Given the mass distribution of prepackaged instructional materials, how will the individual teacher protect his freedom to teach what he believes is most relevant to the needs of his students? As more and more personal information goes into the computer files, the question of invasion of privacy becomes a significant issue (Miller, 1970). Who pays for the high cost of the research and development of educational technology, and especially, who pays for the local services to students and teachers? Once the student pecked out his data analysis on the department's desk calculator, but the tempo of computation is now stepped up by a factor of one million or so! In many departments students are expected to learn how to program a computer and this amounts to a new "language" requirement. Should the institution adopt the library model and absorb the cost of computer services for the entire academic community, or should it follow a pay-for-service policy? If the computer becomes extensively used as a teaching resource, it seems inevitable that computer services must become an institutional responsibility.

Finally, it must be recognized that updated hardware installations and sophisticated instructional "systems" will not, by themselves, bring about optimal use of the technological resources for education. Steps must be taken to correct the basic single deterrent, already stressed in this chapter: the fact that the highest status and academic rewards have customarily been reserved for those faculty members who engage in productive research and who publish books and articles to be read by other discipline specialists. Good teaching has either been taken for granted, or introduced as "evidence" for reward only when a candidate's research output is thought to be marginal. A university is a source of new knowledge as well as one means for its dissemination (teaching). A given member of the faculty cannot be all things by way of research, community service, and teaching, and the reward system of the institution should differentiate, but recognize, the particular contribution of the individual members of the faculty.

Machines and Value Judgments

Students can use technological aids to acquire necessary factual, conceptual, and procedural information on their own and then meet with their teacher in the classroom to discuss the how-comes and the why-fors, and what is being done about them. It would seem to devalue academic currency if a college course for credit were mediated to the students entirely by automated means. There are many such offerings in schools around the country, and their lack of human interaction is a serious limitation. Teachers are needed to promote and to support divergent learning, to avert a drift toward intellectual conformity and educational orthodoxy. Automation can indeed serve a vital function in the university. Not by itself, but as a resource for the teacher who is willing to walk outside the path of least resistance to develop the conditions for learning for his students.

Earlier the library was pointed to as "the technological center of the university." True enough, but this, by itself, is a trivial designation. Archibald MacLeish (1973) knows the meaning of these "manuscripts in bottles" in the life of a school:

> For the existence of a library, the fact of its existence, is, in itself and of itself, an assertion—a proposition nailed like Luther's to the door of time. By standing where it does at the center of the university—which is to say at the center of our intellectual lives—with its books in a certain order on its shelves and its cards in a certain structure in their cases, the true library asserts that there is indeed a "mystery of things." Or, more precisely, it asserts that the reason why the "things" compose a mystery is that they seem to mean: that they fall, when gathered together, into a kind of relationship, a kind of wholeness, as though all these different and dissimilar reports, these bits and pieces of experience, manuscripts in bottles, messages from long before, from deep within, from miles beyond, belonged together and might, if understood together, spell out the meaning which the mystery implies. (p. 359)

Chapter 12

Grading or Evaluation

Academic authority reaches its peak, but not its fulfillment, when the teacher assigns the grade. Grades are administrative shorthand for ranking students against one another and for reporting how well a student has achieved the standards prescribed by the faculty. Evaluation, on the other hand, serves the learner and is indispensable in the learning process. Without some form of evaluative appraisal, learning becomes inefficient; the student loses the guides that enable him to control the direction and the rate of his learning. Evaluation can take the form of conferences between student and teacher, comments on papers and exams, conversations with other students, and the student's own self-criticism. It is the process by which the student is informed of how well he is achieving the goals the teacher has set for the class and those he has set for himself.

The confusion between evaluation and grading reaches ironic proportions at the typical Honor's Day convocation. Whereas alumni are often recognized for the significant and distinctive quality of their individual accomplishments as citizens, scholars, or professionals, undergraduates are rewarded for their

skill in maintaining high grade-point averages: the
3.80s and above get the blue ribbons; the 3.79s go
unnoticed; they need not have come since they, with
the rest of the class, are consigned to mediocrity. In
this instance, the alumni are evaluated, the students
are graded—a distinction that will appear throughout
this chapter.

Measuring Student Achievement

Testing is the most common formal evaluating process, and an old educational aphorism, "The power
to test is the power to control the curriculum," states
clearly enough the criterion function of testing. Regardless of catalog descriptions and in spite of the
teacher's projected objectives stated on the first day
of class, the objectives that count are revealed when
the teacher prepares his examinations or otherwise
indicates the basis on which he will evaluate students. Despite polite phrases about "learning for
learning's sake," students are aware that grades mean
the difference between academic success and disappointment. As a result, they frequently value rote
memorizing above understanding as the best way to
keep their grade-point averages in good shape. It is
unfortunate that testing and grading have become almost synonymous since a well-planned program of
testing can provide discriminating feedback and thus
yield educational benefits to the learner (Ebel, 1973).

Testing—More Than One Function

If they are carefully constructed, tests provide useful
diagnostic information to the teacher. Good tests and
quizzes can also serve as useful *motivators* and provide *instructional* support by helping students to organize and focus their study efforts. Normally, however, no single testing instrument will perform

evaluative, diagnostic, and motivational functions equally well.

Diagnosis. Teachers and students both benefit from a diagnostic test given during the first few weeks of a course. By quizzing students on the major topics he intends to cover and testing the skills he believes are prerequisite for success in his course, the instructor will know more about areas in which his students are already well prepared and in which areas they are weak. Consultation with a psychometric (tests and measurement) specialist is probably useful if sectioning or special instructional treatment will be the consequence of diagnostic testing. Tests can perform diagnostic functions throughout the semester: are students "keeping up," where are they having trouble, who are the laggards, has the class mastered a course segment sufficiently? For diagnostic purposes, information about responses to the individual test items is more helpful to the student than knowing his total test score.

Motivation. Students tend to structure their study habits and classroom attitudes around their expectations of how they will be evaluated. This is made painfully obvious in the barrage of student questions regarding what readings will be covered, what type of questions will be used, and how much the examination will count in the final grade. The burst of studying energy just before an examination (cramming) is the realistic norm among college students. Periodic evaluation during the term, therefore, utilizes this motivational habit by setting frequent short-term goals toward which they can work. The sudden removal of an examination threat frequently leaves students at a loss as to how to spend their time and how to establish self-control over their own program of study. Part of the confusion stems from the cues students take from the teacher, who himself places high emphasis on earning good grades.

Instructional support. Making results available immediately after a test strengthens the instructional value of the exam. If a large number of students are stumped by a question, explaining the correct answer will help them to understand the concept being tested; if several answers were possible, examining the alternatives will increase the student's command of the values implicit to this discrimination. The item-by-item analysis of a carefully made test will indicate whether students are learning what the teacher expects them to learn, the extent to which they understand his presentation, and the use they are making of auxiliary instructional resources, e.g., library references or laboratory projects.

The final exam is often the teacher's most revealing comment on the contribution of his course to the education of his students. If his exam demands only progress in memorizing, facts are probably what most students will learn (for the exam, that is). If, on the other hand, the teacher evaluates students in terms of their ability to apply facts and to synthesize and organize and to manage generalizations, the performance of his students will probably reflect these more intricate criteria of achievement. Good tests of comprehension are, however, especially difficult to prepare (Anderson, 1972).

The Teacher-Made Objective Test

The teacher's good intentions about defining his instructional objectives face the moment of truth when he sits down to put together an evaluating instrument. Defining, organizing, and assessing meaningful instructional goals put the teacher's talent to its most demanding test. The dimensions of his evaluations are telling indicators of what he defines as being educationally worthwhile and should, therefore, carry considerable weight as a measure of his general competence as a teacher.

The teacher who is faced with a class of 100 or more students must find some fair and dependable method of assessing the achievement of each member of the class. For a large class with one teacher and no instructional assistance from others, reading and grading essay exams, term papers, and special projects is altogether too time-consuming, and holding individual conferences is not a realistic possibility. Under these conditions the instructor will probably turn to objective testing.

Formulating questions for an objective exam is a creative but rigorous task. The work is slow—professional exam writers do well if they construct between five and ten good items a day. Questions must be unambiguous, alternative answers must be plausible, and responses must indicate a discriminating level of understanding on the part of the student. Because of the difficulties involved, a teacher would be well advised to begin writing his test long before exam time. The usual criticism of objective testing—the mindlessness of what is actually being measured—can only be countered by careful test development on the part of the teacher. Testing specialists maintain that the objective format can measure to some degree most of the important educational objectives, such as solving problems, recommending action, making predictions, drawing inferences, and evaluating judgmental alternatives. The range of possibilities, they claim, is limited only to the instructor's skill and inventiveness—and his willingness to spend a great deal of time preparing an objective examination.

Under the pressure of an early testing deadline

the teacher may revert to what he believes is a relatively easy type of objective exam—true-false statements. However, few statements are clearly true or false (probably fewer each year). Multiple-choice items, matching items, convergent problem-solving questions, fill-in-the-blank items are generally better than true-false items, but each have their special advantages and limitations. *Recognizing* a right from a wrong answer requires a less thorough degree of learning than does the ability to *recall* specific information. Whether this is a criticism or an advantage of the objective instrument will vary from one testing situation to another, e.g., whether the information itself will likely be needed in a context calling only for recognition, or for the unaided recall of what was learned earlier.

Having invested considerable time in the construction of a complete objective examination, the teacher should use the results of its first administration to "debug" the test. "Item analysis" is a procedure for locating systematic errors and points of weakness and strength in the exam, such as its difficulty level and its discriminating power. Individual items that may be too easy or too hard, or are redundant, or deadwood, can be identified, corrected, or eliminated. Testing the test usually results in a better measuring instrument when students are to be compared against one another—"norm-referenced tests." Successive test revisions should not, however, be based solely on data given by the item analysis. A teacher's professional judgment—"criterion-referenced tests"—about the validity of certain segments of information is the ultimate factor in evaluating what students learn.

Students tend to be wrought up about examinations. While a moderate amount of anxiety may facilitate study and test-taking, a high anxiety level inter-feres with learning and causes poor performance. Since trickery has no place in the evaluation scheme, an open discussion about the examination can help to ease the pressure of exam taking. To confuse or, worse, to mislead students about an examination merely reduces the reliability of a test and weakens the confidence of students in its educational value and in the value of the course as a whole. Testing should not pit teacher against students or students against one another; as a resource for learning, the procedures for evaluation should provide feedback to each student about what is most important in his/her educational progress.

Subjective Evaluation and the Individual Student

Objective testing is planned to be impersonal and this is its strength as well as its weakness. Examinations of this type do not give students the opportunity to redefine a statement, to offer partly correct answers, to introduce original insights, or to answer the important question: "How well am I doing when I'm learning and thinking on my own?" Subjective assessment by the teacher at least has the potential of escaping from the preestablished template and to give students opportunity to express and to defend their own thinking. The bluebook has been familiar fare for college students for a long time, and teachers still keep at it despite the wearisome hours, confident that these tests reveal their students' abilities to organize, synthesize, and draw conclusions from material they have studied. The competence of the teacher is also being tested as he evaluates the evidence, the argument, and the unexpected insights given by the student. If the student was aiming at a worthwhile target, even if different from the teacher's, he can be evaluated in constructive terms and without penalty. This flexibility for personal evaluation is one of the chief advantages of the essay exam, the oral exam, term papers, and special projects; they encourage the expression of independent learning.

The essay exam. The essay exam can range from a series of short completion items to a single question that may demand writing for two hours or two days on a single topic. Its weakness is not in the form of the questions or their purpose; the difficulty lies in reliable scoring. This source of error (inconsistency) is minimized if the questions are sufficiently clear and have enough detail to assure that each student understands the implications intended with the question. Any restrictions as to the scope and length of answers should not be ambiguous. When evaluating essay tests, teachers generally rely more on their immediate recognition of quality than on attempts to be analytically systematic. Evaluating a set of written responses is undoubtedly influenced (perhaps without awareness) by the quality of the answers that have already been read, legibility, fatigue, or other biasing factors. Therefore, teachers who use essay exams should:

1. Ensure that new readers (if readers are used by the teacher in scoring) receive supervised practice in test scoring
2. Score each paper without knowing who wrote it
3. Grade all answers to one question at one sitting
4. Counterbalance or randomize the sequence in which the bluebooks are read for the different questions

It is relatively easy to note those instances where a student is shooting aimlessly or in a blunderbuss fashion, or simply being verbally artistic. The dif-

ficult task for the teacher or reader is to avoid drifting
into a narrow set, and to fail to recognize that some of
the "right" answers may be quite different from the
teacher's original expectation.

Oral exams. The main advantage usually offered
in the face-to-face examination is the flexibility to
pursue in depth some aspect of the examinee's response. From the examiner's view, the student is
being given an opportunity to display quickness of
mind under pressure as well as ingenuity in handling
an unexpected question or query. Attention can also
be given to his personal manner and his nonverbal
means of communicating his feelings, beliefs, and
opinions. These characteristics may themselves be
assessed (rightly or wrongly) as indicators of a student's further success in roles other than as a student.
The prospect of an oral encounter and the "confron-
tation" itself frequently generate considerable anxiety and defensiveness. As a consequence the student
may not appear at his best and may give an inferior
display of what he knows, the way he thinks, and the
personal characteristics that normally mark his manner in less threatening situations of intellectual prob-
ing and review. On the other hand, some students are
highly verbal and self-assured and seem to perform at
their best under such conditions.

Oral exams are frequently conducted by a committee and this group is, itself, a "problem." Each
member is sensitive to his own position and professional status. Differences of opinion often occur, and
examiners sometimes upstage the student. The evaluation procedure will be improved if the committee
members engage in a pretesting session where some
of the role-playing and other sources of confusion can
be gotten out of the way. Ideally, the examiners

should make independent ratings following the session although a group discussion at this time may help to resolve differences and to reach a consensus evaluation.

Term papers and special projects. Writing a term paper or carrying out a special project is a necessary condition for learning in many courses. For a course with a large enrollment, the task of reading and evaluating these products would be excessive for a single teacher. Where the subject matter is not overly technical, students can read and evaluate the work of their peers. The experience of reading and commenting on themes, essays, and reports is a worthwhile educational event itself. The specific procedures for using undergraduate students as readers and the weight given to their evaluations will vary greatly with different kinds of courses. This added responsibility however, usually calls for advanced preparation and supervision by the regular teacher.

Some students prefer a well-structured sequence of assignments; others want freedom to define a special project or at least to select from a list of eligible topics. In either case, the very process of putting together a distinctive unit of knowledge tends to dispel indifference. Pride in the quality of one's work is an almost universal reinforcing condition. The preparation of a paper, or report of a special project, involves several of the primary conditions for effective learning—active participation, selective screening of ideas, the meaningful organization of material, explicit and overt communication, and the intrinsic reward of acquiring new knowledge and understanding. Evaluating such products by the teacher is most effective when it takes the form of running marginal comments, since students benefit more from the qualitative feedback to their succession of ideas than from a single grade entered on the cover page.

Summary

The first part of this chapter has emphasized assessment methods that encourage students to reference data and logic in support of divergent conclusions, to maintain the individual flavor of their learning and thinking. Obviously, where the facts-of-the-matter are firm and are prerequisite to later learning, a good, solid test of how well students have learned what they should learn, is in order.

Despite the value and the convenience of well-constructed psychometric instruments, the era of mass testing of intellectual aptitudes and intellectual achievement may have reached its peak. These scores leave out too much that is important in education and especially do they leave out the idiosyncratic individual. Over thirty-five years ago Gordon Allport (1937) pointed out that personality cannot be measured with scaled testing instruments, and the same limitation applies to the learning and thinking of the individual student.

The pressures of social activism and humanistic education add further strain to the testing, measuring, and classifying tradition. The purposes of protesting and self-actualizing students are difficult to key into a test-scoring machine. In fact, many question the validity of the teacher's role as assessor, believing that persons individually or in a "jury" from the larger community might better evaluate how well a student has defined an issue and how well he "communicates" his analysis. Most will accept the educational value of evaluation. The same cannot be said of grading.

The Assignment of Grades

Measurement requires a reference point, e.g., the atmospheric pressure at sea level, the cost of living in 1960. The "zero" point for the assessment of human performance is usually the average—the average I.Q. is set at 100, the nationally averaged SAT is 500. The conventional course grade and, in summation, the grade-point average take on meaning in reference to an academic norm. Grading implies that such a norm exists, whether it be objective (standardized national norms), or subjective (the teacher's own frame of reference), or a mix of the two (the grade distribution for a particular course).

The reference norms for grades vary from teacher to teacher, from department to department, and from college to college. Despite this variability, formal grades have become the most conspicuous means of assessing student performance. Student preoccupation with the grade as a measure of achievement reflects the preoccupation of teachers with providing a neatly packaged symbol for each student's accomplishment in each course. These assessments are then used (1) by the university to indicate that the student has met its "requirements" for academic rigor; (2) by professional and graduate schools in their selection processes; (3) by potential employers to predict on-the-job performance; (4) by parents to assure that they have received their money's worth; (5) by a parade of unknown (often unauthorized) users ranging from the government to creditors to insurance companies.

The social impact of grades derives from the easy comparison that can be made between one student and others. These simplistic rankings and ratings imply a status label which is distasteful to many students. Students may be perfectly willing to learn what the teacher has to offer and to actually seek his qualitative evaluation of their individual efforts, but they object to being classified and labeled (graded) for public review. Their own words express quite well their reasons for objecting:

> Grading is an institution within an institution, a two-pronged device to divide, by pitting student against student, and to conquer, to raise a competitive animal ready to fill his yoke in the American economic treadmill. (a committee of concerned students)

> Our present education system is developing people who are passive, whose knowledge is closed, whose ways of thinking are rigid and who have no feeling for the process of discovering new knowledge and new answers. The student is rarely given a vote of confidence concerning his ability to know what is best for himself regarding his own academic career. (Nancy L.)

> The child finds himself at school and in sudden competition for teacher approval and grades. If he is able to adjust to the structure and demands of the teacher, he "succeeds." As he continues, he will begin to look outward to gain inner satisfaction. If he conforms, he is accepted and praised. He learns, all too quickly, to judge himself through others' opinions. In this process, many destructive things take place. Conformity destroys his creativity. External reinforcements ruin that beautiful inner curiosity and self-motivation, for the child begins to work for the "gold star" rather than to understand that which he finds intriguing and fascinating. Most disheartening of all, is the effect our system has upon the individual's happiness. Throughout life, he will look for external determinants from which to judge his own self-worth. How many people I have watched struggling with despair,

trying to convince themselves of their own self-worth, even though they did fail in one area or another. All of this is of extreme importance when one asks, "What criteria should be used to evaluate the student?" (Margie L.)

These statements analyze and attack the basic assumptions of grade-oriented instructional systems. Paradoxically, the writers of these papers feel pressed to question the teacher if he assigns a grade of B rather than A. They feel strongly about the need for change, but are thoroughly aware of the realities that prevail. They know that however careful, analytical, and multidimensional the instructor's evaluation of the student, in the eyes of the external reviewer of a transcript of credits, the recorded grade supersedes the evaluation process. The universal equation of grades with excellence, or mediocrity, does not escape the student; he works (not necessarily learns) for grades even as he registers his futile protest against being permanently categorized by a set of code letters. Whether by design or circumstance, the grade itself becomes a yardstick by which one student is measured against others; by its very simplicity, a transcript of grades encourages society to form categorical judgments on a student's potential. It is increasingly obvious as students and faculty members begin to sort through the pros and cons of grading that a re-examination of the underlying issues is long overdue.

The Variety of Grades

What "goes into a grade" varies from teacher to teacher. Some grades include penalties for weak character, cutting classes, being late, overdue assignments, and the like. Others penalize (or favor) the slow starter. The distribution of grades is often chaotic, e.g., "I never give A's to freshmen," and grade distributions between departments also vary, sometimes to the point of embarrassment, if not injustice.

A teacher who assigns grades on a *relative* basis must have in mind an ideal grade distribution. Of the various schemes that have been worked out, the normal probability curve is most often used, hence the expression "grading on the curve." In application, it presumes that a class includes a representative sample of students; the performance of the middle range of students can thus be used to define the average, or C grade.

When grading against *absolute* standards, the performance of each student is evaluated in terms of a predetermined criterion; in theory, every student in a class has a chance to earn an A. Because they are competing against the professor's absolute scale and not against one another, students are presumably free to discuss the course among themselves, to study together, and to help one another learn. In its pure form, this policy almost invites the students to "psych out" the teacher and his grade-giving authority; that is, the student must cue himself to follow the habits of thinking, and to echo the priorities, of the person who makes the final decision about the grade.

A third grading policy is to grade each student in terms of his own progress. A "gain" score, however, is difficult to manage equitably for each of the different students in a class since it requires a fairly accurate measure of individual knowledge and skills at the beginning of the course. Further, the goals must be clearly defined for each student, and the weight given to *rate* of progress and to final *level* of achievement must, in some way, be consistent for all students.

A fourth grading policy is gaining in popularity—the "contract." The teacher sets forth the performance (contract) standards required for the A, B, C, etc., grades. In most instances this is some combination of number of papers, projects, exams, and so forth, completed and adjusted in terms of a measure of quality for each product. The self-paced instructional arrangements described in Chapter 7 involve this system and variations can be applied within the conventional testing and grading courses, i.e., a student "contracting" for an A grade has the option of more than one try at equivalent forms of the examination. What happens when 90 percent of the students contract for an A—and make it? Such findings highlight the need for the institutional analysis of its grading system—the ultimate reference for the meaning of a grade.

Grades and Learning

Teachers often justify grades in terms of their effects on students; the belief, for example, that the desire to achieve a high grade-point average will lead a student to study harder and also to study material he would otherwise neglect. The distinction, however, should be made between study effort and learning benefit; between time spent at the books and knowledge gained for productive application beyond the exam. Effort along either of these lines may or may not be reflected in higher grades. According to studies conducted at Amherst College (Birney, 1964), the amount of effort a student invests in a course (measured by study time and independent pursuit of material) is apparently unrelated to grades. The degree of interest a course evokes is a more important factor.

There is little evidence that using grades to punish students yields significant learning benefits. In fact, the punitive approach to grades often has the effect of reducing the interest in a course, or in an entire field of study. Neither are final grades effective feedback devices. They always come *after;* being informed of his A, B, or C one or two weeks after the end of the term is of little educational consequence to a student. A student may want no more than a general grasp of major issues from an elective course but in his field of concentration such a general overview would not be adequate. What students really seek and what they need are evaluating indicators of their progress as they work their way through a course. Qualitative comments from the instructor about specific points of performance is the essence of his evaluating function.

The faculty is a major point of resistance to change in the grading structure. College teachers are among those who have successfully mastered a grade-oriented instructional system and, in addition to their rational reasons for resisting, are not likely to downgrade a factor so intimately correlated with their professional self-confidence. It is hardly necessary to elaborate on the observation that the instructor's attitudes and values about grading influence his management of the classroom. An instructor who conceives of grades in terms of reward and failure will assign them differently from one who conceives of his evaluation as a means of indicating a student's progress from beginning to end of his course. The instructor who is skeptical about the validity of grades will mark students on a different scale than one who is convinced that grades can be objectively assigned and interpreted. Instructors who spend more contact hours with students probably view grades and grading differently than those who merely lecture to large classes.

Grades and Administrative Management

Grades have become a medium of communication within the campus, between schools, and to society. Graduates, for example, are frequently ranked from top to bottom, but research findings do not support the rank order separations based on decimal point differences between adjacent students. Comparisons between more remote ranks might be meaningful and there is some evidence that when viewed overall, an individual's grades tend to reflect a general level of academic performance; on the average, students tend to achieve at the same levels in different courses. Averaging a student's grades for his different courses may thus compensate for the variable nature of his individual grades; deviations in the judgment of twenty to forty instructors over a college career, *when averaged*, do seem to cancel out, leaving a fairly stable indicator of a student's level of performance. But the grade-point average fails to show in what courses he may have excelled due to special interest and skill. The mix of factors that influences the grade-point average remains unknown. Does the grade average reflect inherent intellectual capability and motivation, possession of relevant information, intellectual curiosity, perceptiveness, analytical power, study habits, the ability to synthesize concepts into higher order abstractions, clarity of exposition and expression? Surely the combination varies from student to student.

Next to the questionnaire, data derived from grades are one of the more convenient ways to analyze the education process. The literature is extensive and most of this research accepts the basic assumptions of the grading system. Statistical summaries of the measurable effects of different selection procedures, curricular plans and instructional methods are built upon the grade-point average as the almost universal criterion for evaluation. To a certain extent this mass of data becomes, itself, part of the rationale for maintaining the conventional system.

Grades have long been used for selecting students for movement up the academic ladder—from high school to college to graduate or professional school, and then on to postdoctoral fellowships and, finally, as a factor in the initial job appointment. As a matter of fact, except for the two ends of the grade distribution, grades are not very good predictors from one level of education to another. The kinds of abilities and the performance measured by teachers at one level differ in some important respects from what teachers grade at the next higher level of education. Since many students drop out or transfer to a different area of study (more often than not, these are the students who have not been doing so well), those who remain, therefore, represent a progressively more selected group; the range of abilities within the group is considerably reduced and this lowers the predictive correlations. There is a fairly high (.55 to .60) correlation of high school grades and achievement test scores with grades in the first semester in college, but ability to predict college grades from high school grades drops regularly in each succeeding college semester (Humphries, 1968).

Thus, the accumulated grade record falls short of being a useful predictor of postgraduate success. According to studies surveyed by Warren (1970) experience on the job and evaluation by supervisors are far more accurate predictors of how "successful" an employee will be than is his college record. Hoyt (1965) reviewed the literature on this point and, after analyzing forty-six different studies, summarized that "college grades bear little or no relationship to any measures of adult accomplishment." This conclusion is surprising, if not shocking, to many of us who have been giving grades to hundreds of students year after year. We tend to overlook the fact that while the capabilities that students bring to campus stay with them after graduation, the criteria for successful performance on the job include many factors other than what classroom grades measure.

Re-Thinking the Grade

Teachers on many campuses are reassessing their assessment procedures. If we choose to speak the language of statistics and averages, we can conclude with Warren (1971) that "grades can be neither damned nor praised with any confidence. . . . They help some students find structure and purpose in their academic pursuits while discouraging others who may be better candidates for learning. . . ." Teachers know that error is partner to passing judgment on the quality of student performance, and the question of educational justice is most clearly posed in matters of grading. A critical reappraisal should be directed not only to the mechanics of our current grading systems, but also to the entire concept of the grade as a useful indicator of student achievement.

Pass-fail grading. Not so long ago faculties were debating whether or not to allow the plus and the minus as "refinements" to the basic letter grade—a far cry from the current debate about the pass-fail option. Pass-fail proponents argue that the two-point system will reduce student anxiety over grades, that a student's efforts will be shifted from gradesmanship to learning. Students will no longer have to compete against one another and against the teacher; learning will become a positive, cooperative venture and students will have greater control over how they will spend their study time. For example, they can take courses that they otherwise might not elect for fear of risking a drop in grade-point average, e.g., science and engineering students taking courses in the humanities. Students accept and appreciate all of these justifications, but, to them, its greater appeal lies as one firm step away from the rank-order categorizing, the coercive learning, and the restraint to open inquiry imposed by the A-through-F pigeonholes for grading.

The research results on the effectiveness of the pass-fail scheme have been inconclusive. In one pilot experiment (Pascal, 1967), it was found that students (not known to the teacher) who elected pass-fail were assigned grades similar to those they had earned under the regular grading system in other courses—A students earned As and B students Bs, and so forth. In another study (Koen, 1972), questionnaire data from 950 students enrolled in fifty-two different sections of a large introductory psychology course showed little support for claims of the pass-fail advocates nor for the counterclaims by those defending the conventional grading system. "Content acquisition was no greater under A-F grading; feedback to students was no more frequent. . . ." It seems evident that old habits of study and gradesmanship are slow to change. Pass-fail students probably "slack off" no more or no less than in a graded course. The appeal and validity of the subject matter and the freedom to follow individual interests are probably more important factors in controlling class attendance and amount of time spent in study.

Nonpunitive grading. Pass-fail grading may be only an interim step toward the less punitive "pass-no record" and "credit-no entry" schemes. Here the student receives credit only for those courses in which he achieves at an acceptable level—the faculty must decide whether the minimum "pass" corresponds to the former C or D level of performance. At any rate, the student is not given a public penalty for life for failing to perform at an adequate level. He is "punished" nonetheless, by the loss of tuition payments, possible delay in graduation, the unproductive use of his time and energy, and the self-realization of failure to achieve a goal. One straightforward way to eliminate punitive grading would be to allow a student to voluntarily "drop" the course at will—including the day of the final examination. The failing grade is the end-product of so many different factors that it is difficult to assign clear meaning to the E or F grade. Only on occasion does it indicate the lack of *ability* to achieve a minimum level of competence in a course of study.

In principle and as a record of achievement (rather than exposure), nonpunitive grading requires that the teacher set explicit goals and devise valid means for evaluating student achievement of these goals. Otherwise, the reporting system serves neither the purpose of a grade or of evaluation; it is simply an indication that the bodies stayed warm and twitched now and then. When used to its full advantage, nonpunitive grading places heavier demands on the teacher than does the conventional course in which he aims to "cover the field" and to grade students in terms of how well their thinking matched his. The teacher denies himself the "threat of failure" as a device for controlling and managing his class and rests his case on the positive appeal of the goals of the course and his ability to recognize and to reward the progress of his students toward these objectives. Under these conditions, the grading system becomes a strong constructive factor in the instructional affairs of the high school, college, or university.

Grading options. Traditionally, the grading system has belonged to the school as its academic currency, which it controls for in-house rewards and for exchange (job placement) with the outside community and with other universities. The question is now being asked whether the separate professional schools and colleges within the large university might better achieve their educational purposes by introducing variations to the standard grading scheme. Within a college the same question is asked by the separate departments and by teachers of subsets of courses at different levels within the department. Should the teacher control the grading policy for his own course and should students have options as to how they will be graded?

The whole matter soon becomes complicated, and the agenda of faculty-student committees on grading must include the issue of local options as they discuss the different grading policies and practices. If the option principle is accepted, the immediate question is whose option takes precedence and what are the available alternatives? The debate can become quite trying but is extremely important nonetheless since the discussion is aimed at the standards that define the meaning of the formal educational process as perceived by students, faculty, and the community at large.

Argument for Grading System

The main defense of grades—and it is a strong one—is their usefulness in the management of the educational enterprise. Precisely because higher education has acquired a strong dependency on grades, it will not quickly forsake them as its medium of exchange. And yet communicating what a student has accomplished to agencies beyond the classroom serves a purpose quite different from meeting the instructional needs of the student. If outside institutions (industry, government, and professional organizations) require an appraisal of students or graduates, the burden of establishing the criteria for these evaluations should be placed on these institutions and not on the universities from which the students graduate. Comparative rankings of different applicants or candidates can probably be made by these outside groups in a more equitable fashion for their own purposes than by comparing grade-point averages. Within the campus itself grade-point averages provide the basis for many management-type decisions, but a faculty debate on grading should make a clear distinction between matters of administrative convenience and ways to improve grading as a resource for learning.

In the light of the research evidence on the differential effects of reward and punishment on learning—and this is the main thrust of research related to the *instructional* value of grades—the most significant single change in the conventional grading system would be to eliminate the punitive failing grade. An A, B, C, No-entry system would allow the student, in effect, to drop a course at any time. The "drop" carries its own punitive consequences and, thus, the evaluating efforts of the teacher can be aimed almost exclusively toward informing students as to their status with respect to the quality of performance required by the A, B, or C grade. Under these conditions the grading system becomes a constructive factor.

It seems unlikely that there will be any rapid solution to the problem of grading. Grading touches too many people, serves too many purposes, and is a controlling criterion for too much of the educational process. Nevertheless, an institution might forsake its role as quality controller for society and devise alternative means for recording and reporting academic achievement, and especially for providing evaluative information to each student during the actual course of progress toward particular educational goals.

Chapter 13

The Apprentice Teacher

The spotlight now moves from the student to the teacher—his preparation for entry into this career and the influences that shape the nature of his performance as a teacher. Most college teachers start out as graduate student teaching assistants and the in-service preparation of the beginning teacher is gradually coming about. The analysis of these programs helps to clarify the important elements in effective college teaching generally.

Orientation and Training

For the first time in a long time, the supply of teachers exceeds the demand. In the competition for available openings more weight is now given to the teaching competence of the candidate, and university graduate departments realize that the research credentials of the Ph.D. graduate may not, by themselves, be sufficient for successful entry into a career of college teacher. The Doctor of Arts (D.A.) degree programs are being developed as an alternative which gives special emphasis to training as a teacher. In response, the Ph.D. proponents take the position that research training is a necessary component for the college teacher and, further, the specific skills of teaching can be acquired within the Ph.D. program. In any case, ideas and procedures for the preparation of the college teacher are centering around the graduate student teaching assistant—the TA.

The Status of the Teaching Assistant

The TAs found their place in the academic sun following World War II when they were seen as a source of cheap labor to meet expanding undergraduate enrollments. They became a relatively permanent part of the instructional force, but were given little preparation for college teaching. In fact, the very existence of these younger teachers was soft-pedaled to avoid the charge that high academic standards of instruction were being compromised. Even today some private universities are still "holding the line" against graduate student teaching assistants.

Granted, experience and scholarly and scientific maturity lead to better teaching but this does not rule out the use of teaching assistants, especially if they are carefully selected, trained, and supervised in their instructional assignments. Both the research evidence (usually based on student ratings) and the experience of colleges using TAs indicate that these younger teachers are a valuable resource for maintaining the quality and the flexibility of a department's instructional program. The main problem is to find the best ways to select, train, and supervise these apprentice teachers for their classroom responsibilities.

Koen and Ericksen (1967) conducted a survey to locate noteworthy examples of TA training programs among the 50 larger universities that produce the most Ph.D.s. Based on the responses to the initial inquiry, 20 universities were selected for visits and detailed interviews were conducted with 105 department chairmen, TA supervisors, and other faculty members. In most of these training programs virtually all relevant activity was initiated by and confined to the discipline departments. Almost half of the training programs had remained in substantially their present form for ten years or more although during this time, undergraduate enrollment in almost every institution had just about doubled, as had the number of TAs employed.

In about one third of the departments there appeared to be no overall supervision of training; instead, each faculty member provided such supervision and guidance as he saw fit for his own TAs. It is significant that in less than one third of the observed programs was faculty time expressly set aside for the supervising function. In the remainder, supervision of TAs was simply added on to a faculty member's other administrative, teaching, and scholarly activities. "Methods" courses appeared to be a universal anathema and almost one third of the departments implicitly took the position that the apprentice teacher learns to structure the pedagogical issues for himself and to work out his own solutions. One can conclude that in the middle 1960s the universities had made relatively few administrative adjustments and even fewer time commitments toward assuming formal responsibility for training the apprentice college teacher.

Perhaps the most significant positive findings of the survey were: (1) The special influence on the quality of a training program of an individual member of a department faculty who perceived the task of preparing the beginning teacher as a necessary and worthwhile effort and who, in turn, received support and backing from the important figures in the academic hierarchy. (2) The demonstrated success of advanced and experienced TAs serving as guides and mentors for the first- and second-year teaching assistants.

Guides for a Training Program

College teaching has become so complex that the beginning teacher will nearly always benefit from a period of supervised preparation as he moves to the other side of the desk. It is also clear that individual departments will go about this task in quite distinctive ways. There cannot be just one training program applied *in toto* in all departments; preparation for teaching biology, for example, is different from what is required for teaching history, mathematics, sociology, and so forth. Without compromising the significance of these differences, certain general features can be specified as points of reference for a department-based program of supervised training for the apprentice teacher. No single "model" for the training of teachers will go very far or last very long, but certainly if teacher training or supervision is assigned to someone "in addition to your other duties," the program will probably not be successful. The orientation and preparation of the apprentice teacher, like the quality of teaching itself, will sooner or later reflect the reward structure of the department.

Support and involvement by the department. The research findings and the experiences of many departments show that the stance of the department leadership and of the senior faculty toward the importance of good teaching is a significant factor in the operation of an effective training program. This stance is demonstrated in several ways, namely, comparable stipend rates for TAs and research assistants, the quality of supervision available to these new teachers, and the continuity of teaching-related values and programs from one year to the next. A 1970 survey of over 500 teaching assistants at the University of Michigan (Brown, 1972) and a comprehensive report from the University of Minnesota (Anderson and Berdie, 1972) both showed that teaching assistants are, as a group, critically discriminating about the strengths and weaknesses of their experiences as beginning teachers. Typically, their strongest reservations had to do with salary, participation in the governance of the department, and inadequate supervision with respect to their specific teaching task. Despite these reservations, however, they appreciate the opportunity to gain on-the-job experience as preparation for the teaching career.

Two department-level actions have an important influence on the climate of the training program:

1. *A policy statement on the role of TAs.* Considerable confusion exists among beginning teachers with respect to their role, status, responsibilities, rights and privileges. For example, how much classroom autonomy can the TA expect? In the absence of an explicit policy statement by the department, serious misunderstandings and bitterness may develop, or the TAs may perceive their task mainly as a job or money-earning assignment rather than a professional opportunity and responsibility. Policy statements as to the status of TAs are also needed at the level of the college and the university. Taken together, these policy statements serve as a guide to decision making and to action with respect to TAs in comparison with other functions graduate students perform. For example, graduate students and faculty are both fully aware of the teaching/research conflict—higher reward priority to research but more personal satisfaction in teaching (Miller and O'Con-

nor, 1972). Written evidence as to the department reward system for teaching would be regarded with suspicion but with keen interest nonetheless.

2. *Selection.* The recruitment of new graduate students and their assignment as TAs, research assistants, or to a service function, e.g., counselor, are normally made at the department level and in line with its overall needs and the available resources for student support.

The beginning teacher has been spectator to the teaching process for many years and has witnessed, firsthand, many different styles and has favored some over others. The influence of his teachers became more pronounced as he moved through one course after another within his specialty field and when, in his own mind, he began to think of himself as a teacher. A department that is free to select its most interested and qualified students for the teaching role holds a potential advantage in maintaining its standards of teaching. Over and over again, ratings of "good teaching" stress personal characteristics such as: interest in students, enthusiasm for the subject, tolerance toward divergent opinions, and sensitivity to the feelings of students. These attributes of good teachers are not greatly changed one way or another through supervision or formal instruction on how to be a teacher. Self-selection will by no means guarantee successful teaching, but it will screen out students who already have reason to believe that teaching is not their cup of tea.

The training program itself. Data on whether a formal training program will provide better teachers are not easily found (Centra, 1972), although those who have participated in such a program report that they feel better prepared to teach than do those who have not. The following suggested program is flexible and identifies only those factors which have been found to be workable and feasible.

1. *Preservice orientation.* The specific responsibilities of the training supervisors usually start with one or more sessions aimed at providing the *information* needed by the new teachers about the policies and procedures that characterize the school and the department. The presession is the appropriate time to distribute handbooks and reading lists related to the nature of college teaching in general and the special demands of teaching within a particular discipline. Certain journals in most of the major disciplines give emphasis to problems and new developments in teaching. The publications in "higher education" are extensive but most of these journals and books are aimed at the professional rather than to apprentice teachers in a subject-matter field.

A large university provides a variety of instructional resources (media facilities, testing and examination bureaus, counseling and reading improvement centers, libraries, etc.) and every new teacher should know where to find and how to utilize these services. Despite the temptation to offer lectures on good teaching, the preservice sessions better serve the purposes of orientation. The specific skills of teaching and the development of one's self-concept as a teacher are the focus of the inservice program.

2. *Inservice training.* Some departments have had considerable experience with teacher training while others have given less attention to this task. The interaction between TAs and their supervisors is generally oriented around on-the-job experiences. The beginning teacher, however, nearly always likes

to talk things over with his peers and the brown-bag discussion group is a likely setting for directing the training program, since the agenda is intimately tied to concrete experiences. A formal course "covers the ground" efficiently but tends to analyze the teaching function in terms of abstract conceptual categories rather than to focus on the person-to-person interactions that concern the apprentice teacher. These group discussions (a teaching seminar) should, nevertheless, be planned around the major objectives of the formal training program. The following five features are sufficiently general to be applicable to most department-based programs. These are overlapping objectives rather than discrete units to be treated one at a time.

a) Acquisition of *competence in the skills of teaching* required for the initial teaching assignment—lecturing, leading a discussion group, tutoring, defining course objectives, and so forth. This is the kernel of the training program. The distribution of time and effort should be determined by the needs of the apprentice teacher. On-the-job training in these skills is the most essential single feature and is where the beginner with little or no experience needs closest supervision and support as he combines observation with part-time teaching.

b) Discussion and demonstration of the *general techniques, procedures, and media for teaching*—the advantages and limitations of technological aids, the use of residential and community resources, role playing, the principles of good testing and evaluation, student participation in the instructional process, and so forth. The emphasis will vary according to the resources available and the special requirements of the discipline area, but the new teacher should at least know about the major resources generally used by college teachers and participate in sample demonstrations.

c) Discussion of the basic conditions for learning, motivation, and attitude and value changes of students. These topics focus more on the *student as a learner* than on the teacher as a giver of information; they link the classroom with selected contributions from psychological research and theory. The principles involved are general, but if applications and illustrations can be taken from the TA's experience as a student and teacher, he will be able to distinguish superficial instructional fads from the more significant conditions that influence the academic progress of students.

d) Competence and fairness in testing and grading are necessary for good teaching. A case can be made that it is hardly ethical for beginning teachers to make formal assessments about the performance of students without being aware of the major factors that distort these judgments. A careful analysis of the nature and process of *evaluation* is a necessary component in the preparation of the apprentice teacher.

e) Discussion of issues associated with the *teaching career*—academic freedom, education and social change, institutional decision making with its reward system and resistance to change. TAs are a new generation of teachers and their priority values must be recognized as they explore beliefs about teaching with a group of equally involved peers. This is less an agenda item for the teaching seminar than a quality within the program which encourages each TA to develop a *personal style and identity* as a teacher within an atmosphere of support, understanding and trust.

3. *Supervision.* Classroom visitation by a senior member of the faculty is a traditional form of super-

vision but this practice needs to be rather carefully reconsidered. A good training program requires considerably more constructive guidance about specific teaching practices than is customarily given. In a follow-up study of career teachers who were asked to evaluate their earlier training as TAs (Miller, 1973), the value of class visitation was judged of "low importance." Familiar beliefs prevail, however, since over three-fourths of those who had never been visited believed that a faculty visit would have been a useful experience in their development as teachers.

In a large department with many teaching assistants, the distinction should be made between the administrative "coordinator" and those who serve as counselors, mentors, consultants for the apprentice teacher. The first-year teacher needs the most counsel and direction, which at this stage should stay rather close to the nuts and bolts of teaching. Discussion of more abstract issues, policies, procedures can come later in the year, preferably in a group setting with the supervisor and other TAs. In a cooperative and congenial atmosphere these TAs will ask for help when needed and a response from the mentors should always be available.

Certain advanced graduate students show considerable enthusiasm toward teaching; they have learned how to organize a body of knowledge, how to design a course, and how to present it successfully to students. They are good teachers and many departments have found that they perform well as advisers and consultants for first-year teachers. Their appointment to this role should be perceived as recognition of merit and one of the more genuine indications of this respect is participation in department decision making and governance.

A growing "supervisory" practice is to use a video-tape replay of a teacher's performance. The use of this technology reduces the dependence on classroom visitation as an arrangement for training, supervision, or evaluation. Seeing oneself at work in front of a class is not a comfortable experience for veterans and is even more disturbing for the beginner. Self-consciousness is lessened if this procedure has been agreed upon and is participated in by several members of the "viewing" group in turn. It is a good ice-breaker since it is the rare individual, indeed, who leaves the television monitor a winner. The procedure is limited, however, in that it tends to focus attention on stylistic mannerisms to the neglect of other and perhaps more important functions of the teacher. Tapes may be available showing a more experienced teacher in action, or a selected tape vignette which demonstrates a particular aspect of teaching.

Evaluating a department-based training program. One direct way of getting information is simply to ask the TAs whether their training has been worthwhile. Feedback of this type will be more helpful if the questions call for comparisons of different features of the training program; if the judgments are focused toward the program rather than toward oneself. Also, these inquiries should be made at several points—at the end of the first and second years of apprentice teaching, and if possible after a year or two of career teaching since the rankings of first-things-first often change as a teacher looks back on the pitfalls and peaks in his development. In a study of 152 first-year "alumni" of TA training programs from ten different departments, Doris Miller (1973) found that these former TAs rated the following experiences as *highly important:*

1. Having total responsibility for a course they had taught
2. Preparation and delivery of a lecture

3. Designing their own exams for their students
4. Informal discussion with other TAs on teaching problems
5. Evaluation of their teaching skill by their students

As an interesting sidelight, 25 additional respondents who had *not* been TAs as graduate students were asked, "On the whole, how helpful were the experiences you had at Michigan in preparing you to be a college teacher?" Only 28 percent indicated that their Michigan experience was a "moderate" or "large" factor in preparing them for college teaching compared to 84 percent among those who had TA experience.

One persistent source of breakdown in a department-based training program is the lack of continuity in leadership from one year to the next. The senior faculty member assigned to conduct the training program will certainly favor his own conception of how the task should be accomplished. It is not so much a question of whether his views are right or wrong as it is whether he is aware of the specific nature of the changes he is introducing, their effects on the participants, and his willingness to discuss and to justify the new procedures. The matter of continuity is therefore a central point for evaluation since a program can quickly become unhinged if the new director insists that everyone start from scratch and follow a new format. The leadership should of course change from time to time and a program must be flexible, but the transition itself requires considerable discussion and advance planning.

Summary. Professor Frank Koen was the prime mover in the five-year, five-department, teacher training project at the University of Michigan. His experience is neatly summarized by the following thirteen questions which pinpoint specific attributes of good training programs and can, therefore, be used as a guide for evaluation. Answers to these questions will vary in detail from one department to another, and each unit will add features that characterize its own program.

1. What is the department's explicit policy statement concerning the role, status, responsibility, and the rights and privileges of the teaching fellow?
2. Insofar as a given department is free to select only certain graduate students as its TAs, on what basis will this selection be made?
3. Who will supervise the TAs participating in the training program—faculty or senior teaching assistants or both? On what basis will these supervisors be selected? How will their participation be credited as a significant proportion of their "teaching load"?
4. What kind of reference materials are available for individual reading and/or as a basis for group discussion?
5. What are considered to be the primary skills of an undergraduate teacher and how does the training program contribute to strengthening these skills?
6. What kinds of teaching and "learning management" techniques is the training program designed to develop (e.g., open classroom, grading options, use of buzz groups, simulation and role-playing, etc.)?
7. How does the reward system within the department recognize and support the teaching function of TAs and faculty in comparison, for example, with research activities?
8. By what intra-department mechanism will continuity be maintained? By what means can each new faculty coordinator or supervisor benefit from and build on what has been learned the past year and the year before, etc.?

9. By what means will the program recognize the special needs of the individual TA?

10. What are the provisions within the program for facilitating greater autonomy and responsibility to the TA as he gains in experience?

11. What criteria will be used to assess the effectiveness of each TA? How will this information be obtained?

12. How does the department propose to utilize the other resources and units within the university relative to the preparation of the new college teacher?

13. What kind of evidence will be sought for evaluating the strengths and the weaknesses of the proposed training program?

Institutional Support

The scope and the quality of a training program reflect the stance of the sponsoring department and this, in turn, is a measure of the support the institution as a whole gives to the teaching function. The first request from most departments to the central administration is for more money and, of course, there is almost no end to the different ways money might be used in the different departments to improve their preparation of apprentice teachers. More often than not, however, one necessary expense is the released time of an experienced teacher to carry out the supervisory function. In the five-year, five-department project at the University of Michigan, the most distinctive and valued use of central funding was to provide the released time of faculty and advance-level TAs to serve as supervisors—guides and mentors for the beginning teachers. Over a period of time this "extra" expense should be absorbed as a normal budget commitment by the department for meeting its obligation for the preparation of its graduates for careers as teachers.

A central agency, such as the Office of the Dean of the Graduate School, in cooperation with the individual departments, should consider how a TA's training and teaching performance can be made a part of his record. These credentials *as a teacher* would be available to prospective employers in a coherent and systematic form. A listing of specific teaching experiences, formal and/or informal training involvement, special skills and interests as a teacher would be a valuable supplement to the usual record of courses taken, grades, publications, and the like. Provision of such credentials would provide tangible evidence that the quality of teaching and the preparation of teachers are, jointly with research capabilities, matters of purposeful concern at the university.

The institutional responsibility for the career development of its faculty *as teachers* has been neglected. This results partly from the higher regard given to research, and also from the general lack of agreement as to "what is good teaching." In committees, workshops, seminars, and forums, faculty members are looking closely at what they do and what they might do as teachers. These discussions frequently start with attention to the technological aids, new methods of teaching, the grading controversy, class size, and the use of graduate student teaching assistants, but sooner or later the hidden agenda will surface, namely, to what extent does the reward system of the institution support efforts to improve teaching? Established teachers are just as sensitive to the supporting climate of the school as are the TAs within a department.

Any college or university worth the tuition it

charges must do something about the topsy-turvy distortion of the resources and the rewards necessary to develop and to maintain its best possible educational program. The establishment of a well-planned program to support the needs of its teachers would evidence institutional good faith. The original rationale for the "summer off" and the sabbatical leave was to enable the professor to improve himself as a teacher, but no single project would by itself be sufficient—faculty retreats to talk about teaching, reward recognition for outstanding teachers, or a formal inservice training program. Much more is needed to ensure the career development of the faculty, that is, to keep teaching up to date and effective without accelerating instructional costs. In general, such a program should include:

1. Access to information about new developments related to teaching
2. Access to new teaching resources—media, computers
3. Funds for instructional experimentation
4. Consultation for the design and evaluation of teaching projects
5. Opportunities for open discussions with peers about values related to teaching—interdisciplinary faculty forums

The length and the ordering of this list will vary from school to school, department to department, and teacher to teacher; thus, the career development of teachers is very closely tied to a multidimensional institutional program of support for better instruction.

Evaluating Teaching

Teaching is an omnibus profession and care must be taken to establish the criteria appropriate for *each* instructional setting and to judge the teacher within this context. The manner and style for successful science teaching would probably be less effective when applied to a descriptive discipline. Some teachers do a better job in a large lecture course than in a discussion group and some have opposite talents; a good tutor may be a poor laboratory instructor. Evaluation is most meaningful when it is specific to a given purpose and recognizes the particular conditions within which the teacher does his job.

The three basic dimensions of teaching as stated earlier are defining the goals and organization of the course, maintaining an optimal classroom environment, and evaluating student performance. A carefully developed evaluating instrument should include items covering all three of these functions. Certainly, a measure of a teacher's "popularity" has little meaning in the absence of reasons for his popularity.

And yet one should not develop false expectations from even the most sophisticated techniques for evaluating teaching. The basic parameters of the teaching function are not yet agreed upon and for this reason it is very often referred to as "an art." To be complete, an evaluating procedure must be explicit as to the criteria involved in reaching the final value judgment. To what extent, for instance, is the evaluation based on a comparison against group norms and are these norms relevant? How careful is the distinction between ratings of the course and ratings of the teacher as an individual, and what about short- and long-term effects? Many such questions should be asked since conclusions drawn from any evaluation procedure are intrinsically bound to the source of information—questionnaires, letters of recommendation, on-site observations, appraisal of instructional end products, review of teaching-related activities, and the like. If these ratings are accepted by the department and/or the institution as a measure of one's teaching success, the mechanics of evaluation very quickly take on a shaping influence as to how the teacher goes about doing his job. If he is "teaching for the test" he is likely to restrain experimentation and inhibit new classroom ventures which may not "fit" the items in the rating form.

Evaluation serves a number of purposes. Students seek information about teachers and courses when planning their program of study. The teacher seeks feedback for improving his course and his teaching relation with students. The focus of most attention and debate, however, is evaluation for purposes of promotion to the tenured rank. The younger teacher reaches the point of "up or out," and opinion is divided as to the prediction of his career contribution to the institution. The complexities of reaching such a decision have almost eliminated the merit promotion from public education in favor of advancement on a seniority basis.

The Administration's View of Teaching

Good teaching is not necessarily correlated, plus or minus, with conformity to administrative criteria. Deans, teachers, and students each view the educational scene from their own vantage point. The question is: What *are* the local values to which the aspiring young teacher should conform? Institutional totems and taboos are often difficult to define, but the beginning teacher must be perceptive to the signals that alert him to the reward system of his department and his school. What is the relative importance, for example, of research, service, and teaching—the usual three dimensions for evaluating faculty members in a university? And more specifically, how does the administration weight: classroom popularity, curricular updating, student counseling, tutorial efforts, committee work, and supervision of research by students?

Colleges and professional groups frequently take special steps to recognize their outstanding teachers. The single "annual award" has the effect, however, of continuing the stereotype of an undifferentiated and undefined teaching mystique. In some instances these recognition awards may be "tokenism" rather than reflecting the reward system that actually prevails at the institution. A practice of making multiple awards would more quickly bring attention and recognition to the significant contributions made by college teachers by means other than their classroom style. Curriculum updating, for example, should be a consideration of recognition, as well as the development of a distinctive program of instruction, or finding ways to utilize new educational resources—as how might a commuter college compensate for the missing residential experience of its students.

Peer Judgments

Among his peers a teacher's reputation takes shape from an accumulation of incidents and comments during the normal course of department affairs. Peer judgments are interlaced with the values of the discipline, i.e., research, professional productivity, and leadership. One's classroom style may not be known or given much weight by fellow department members nor are the criteria for successful academic performance posted on the bulletin board or encoded in a set of bylaws. These standards grow and take form as traditions of the department develop and accommodate to the many variations in teaching. Since there can be no one prototype of the ideal college teacher, these "common law" criteria are probably to be preferred to a strained listing of the defining characteristics of good teaching.

A good number of the researching faculty members who were on "The Flight From Teaching" (Gardner, 1964) are now on the return flight. External research money is less plentiful, and these tenured professors are going back, full time, on the hard-money budget as classroom teachers of undergraduate students. Some interesting things have happened to these classrooms during their absence. For one thing, it is considerably more difficult now to be a "good teacher"—the criteria have changed and are more demanding. The successful teacher has less recourse to the protection of his rank or the "stage tricks" within a single mode of teaching, but most disturbing is the unwillingness of students to sit quietly as anonymous seat numbers. In several ways the new styles of teaching are quite far removed from the conservative authoritarianism of an elite group of elder academic statesmen, and yet these are the men (usually men) whose "peer" judgments are most decisive in controlling the career progress of the younger teachers in the department. As a consequence of budget cuts and relatively modest enrollment increases, fewer younger teachers are receiving appointments to established departments; the average age of the faculty is going up (in some departments almost one year per year) and the resistance to change may become stronger. As a counterbalance, the institution should insist that the evaluation and reviewing mechanism be modified to include the opinions of younger teachers and at least the consensus views of undergraduate and graduate students. Several years ago a cartoon caption said "If the Edsel had been developed by a university faculty, they would still be making it."

Evaluation by Students

Teachers don't like to be graded any more than do their students but students have opinions about a teacher's influence, and their evaluative judgments are relevant to the total picture. The results of such ratings are as reliable (self-consistent) as are most educational assessments. The technical development of teacher-rating scales and their use have not, however, received as much research attention as the complexity of the problem deserves. Costin, Greenough, and Menges (1971) reviewed many of the published reports on student ratings and while the evidence is rarely uniform and unequivocal, they conclude:

> . . . that the criteria used by students in their ratings of instructors had much more to do with the quality of the presentation of material than with the entertainment value of the course per se. Such attributes as preparedness, clarity, and stimulation of students' intellectual curiosity were typically mentioned by students in describing their best instructors . . . Other correlates of student ratings which were noted were: majors tended to rate courses more highly than non-majors in some cases; students required to take a course sometimes rated it lower than those for whom it was an elective; upper class students occasionally gave higher ratings than underclassmen; and experienced or higher ranking instructors usually received higher ratings than did their less experienced colleagues. (p. 530)

The instructor is cautioned to interpret the ratings he receives against three of the more frequent sources of error: (1) The distortion inherent in the selection of aspects-to-be-rated and the words and phrases used in the item statements—do these items include the teacher's primary concerns? (2) The strong halo effect that usually exists. Most students are quite generous in their evaluations and the ratings tend to pile up on the high side. (3) The fact that unless all of the students in the course complete the questionnaire, the instructor will likely receive a biased sample of opinions.

The younger teacher may be disturbed by the fact that despite his best efforts and despite the high ratings he receives from a significant number of students, others in the class see things differently and he is downgraded on several items. These "contrary opinions" have informational value for the teacher. He learns that he cannot be an across-the-board successful teacher; that students differ in their interactions with the teacher, the subject matter, and with their peers. At this point he should be reminded that his own judgment of himself as a teacher may be somewhat biased (Centra, 1972) and further, this feedback from students does not generally result in dramatic changes in his classroom performance. The information received may not match up with the teacher's own needs.

A single questionnaire is not likely to serve the purposes of the administration (for promotion and pay), of students (as a guide for course selection), and of the teacher (as a basis for improving his teaching). These different functions call for particular evaluation procedures but each evaluation in turn will only sample the integrated resourcefulness of the good teacher.

Good Teachers

Good teachers are found in many different settings and have many different ways of doing their job;

there is no single model of the Master Teacher; the search should be ended and the stereotype laid away.

Pedagogical Imprinting

First impressions are important and on the first day of class, students begin to form judgments as to whether or not they have a good teacher. Young adults have already learned the business of being a student; they know the tactics and strategies for the proper management of teachers and they have opinions about the qualities of a good teacher. Teachers know this and old pros as well as rookies walk into the classroom for the first meeting of the term with mixed feelings of anticipation. What are his students looking for in a good teacher? In detail, answers vary, but more often than not students want to know:

1. *Does the teacher care and is he fair?* An instructor who has no particular interest in students as persons, whose primary interest is research rather than teaching and who looks on his classes as forced obligations will soon generate a gap between himself and his students. Regardless of his platform style, if he doesn't care, neither do the students. If his indifference extends to the subject he is teaching, the class is almost doomed to flounder. Students are more likely to object to unfair treatment than to heavy demands in the form of assignments and work load. Fairness with respect to evaluation is frequently a sensitive point. But they also observe whether the teacher is biased or fair when passing judgment about the values of his discipline and the performance of his peers.

2. *Does the teacher know the subject matter?* Students are critical judges of an instructor's subject-matter competence. With practice a teacher may develop various techniques for bluffing, buffering, or

bamboozling on topics about which he feels insecure, ignorant, or indifferent. Whether these techniques are ever appropriate is a matter for individual judgment, but it is doubtful that incompetence in the subject matter one teaches can long be covered up by compensatory tactics.

3. *Is the course relevant to value judgments?* Will this course help me understand the world around me or is it geared to prepare the future subject-matter specialist? Students are asking critical questions about old values and are reassessing the personal meaning and social utility of what they are asked to learn. Does the teacher think seriously about the whole process of what he teaches and its justification? What values does he hold as a teacher-citizen?

Final Impressions

To observe a teacher in action is to be reminded again of the personal quality of teaching, a quality that tends to be passed over in the face of research analyses, technical developments, statistical summaries, questionnaire ratings, and abstracted generalizations about learning theory and college teaching. To some, Mr. Chips, as friend and counselor, is the image of the model teacher. Others give greater weight to charismatic classroom performance—the power to "communicate" to passive listeners, to arouse and stir them up. Teaching is not preaching, and it is certainly not showmanship. The apprentice teacher sees on every hand that the relevance of the message is more important than the polish of the medium.

My own recollection of a good teacher nearly always comes to mind as a counterbalance when reading or hearing about Master Teacher models:

Professor Jones' field was comparative neurology. It is not likely that he ever won an institutional award for outstanding teaching, but within the coordinates of the learning model he was, indeed, a good teacher. He thoroughly enjoyed his subject but his enthusiasm peaked with the nervous system of the earthworm. His knowledge and his excitement about the physiological, biochemical, and behavioral implications of comparative neurology seemed to his students to have no limits. On any one or all of seven days of a week his students could knock on his door—home or office—to receive help or simply to talk about biology or medicine or neurology, but especially to talk about the earthworm and what makes him such a Very Important Person in the biological scale of things.

Professor Jones was a truly influential teacher, although his teaching repertoire included none of the contrived signs of being interested in his students. He liked his students, but this was taken for granted. By precept and by example his students learned the essential meaning of comparative neurology, and they continued this course of study in medicine or zoology or comparative psychology. Professor Jones had neither instructional flair nor classroom style. He mumbled and we strained to hear him; his discourse was often blocked with "ahaaaaaa" and we helped him find the right word; his blackboard sketches needed, and received, corrections. There was no apology in his honest belief that from the one small section of the curricular cafeteria where he was standing could be found amazing knowledge, and he was more than willing and able to help any student for whom the acquisition of this knowledge would be its own reward.

Higher education can always use more "earthworm professors": teachers who present the intrinsic challenge of learning as the major motivating influence in the academic lives of students; teachers who like ideas and students more than they like "teaching"; teachers who have a deep and pervasive identification with their discipline and the curiosity to know more, and who share these qualities openly and generously with their students. These are the important conditions for learning, and therefore, for teaching the young adult.

References

Allen, L. E. 1962. Wiff'n proof: the game of modern logic. New Haven, Conn.: Autotelic Instructional Materials.

Allen, L. E., Rugel, P., and Ross, J. 1970. Queries and theories. New Haven, Conn.: Autotelic Instructional Materials.

Allport, G. W. 1937. *Personality*. New York: Henry Holt.

Anastasio, E. J., and Morgan, J. S. 1972. *Factors inhibiting the use of computers in instruction*. Princeton, N.J.: EDUCOM: Inter-university Communications Council, Inc.

Anderson, J. F., and Berdie, D. R. 1972. *Graduate assistants at the University of Minnesota*. Minneapolis: University of Minnesota, Measurement Services Center.

Anderson, R. C. 1972. How to construct achievement tests to assess comprehension. *Review of Educational Research* 42 (2):145–70.

Ashby, E. 1967. Machines, understanding, and learning: reflections on technology in education. *The Graduate Journal*, 7 (2). Austin, Texas.

Atkinson, J. W. 1964. *An introduction to motivation*. Princeton, N.J.: Van Nostrand.

Atkinson, J. W., and Birch, J. D. 1970. *The dynamics of action*. New York: John Wiley.

Atkinson, J. W., and Feather, N. T., eds. 1966. *A theory of achievement motivation*. New York: John Wiley.

Ausubel, D. P. 1968. Is motivation necessary for learning? In *Educational psychology, a cognitive view*, pp. 364–67. New York: Holt, Rinehart, and Winston.

Axelrod, J. 1970. Teaching styles in the humanities. In *Effective college teaching*, ed. W. H. Morris, pp. 38–53. Washington, D.C.: American Council on Education.

Bandura, A. 1971. Vicarious and self-reinforcement processes. In *The nature of reinforcement*, ed. R. Glaser. New York: Academic Press.

Barron, F. 1969. *Creative person and creative process*. New York: Holt, Rinehart, and Winston.

Berlyne, D. E. 1960. *Conflict, arousal, and curiosity*. New York: McGraw-Hill.

Birney, R. C. 1964. The effects of grades on students. *Journal of Higher Education* 25:96–98.

Bishop, R. 1972. Abstract cited in *Memo to the Faculty*, no. 50. Ann Arbor: The University of Michigan, Center for Research on Learning and Teaching.

Blackburn, R. 1968. Live and learn? A look at students in their setting. *Memo to the Faculty*, no. 32, December, 1968. Ann Arbor: The University of Michigan, Center for Research on Learning and Teaching.

Bloom, B. S., ed. 1956. *Taxonomy of educational objectives: Handbook I cognitive domain*. New York: Longmans, Green.

Blum, R. 1971. Report on innovations in physics education at institutions of higher learning. Preliminary report on the Conference on Priorities for Physics Education, Brief No. 10, Commission on College Physics.

Bordin, E. S. 1969. The teacher as a counselor. *Memo to the Faculty*, no. 38, December, 1969. Ann Arbor: The University of Michigan, Center for Research on Learning and Teaching.

Bowen, H. R. 1972. Can higher education become more efficient? *Educational Record* 53 (3):191–200.

Bowers, D., and Seashore, S. 1969. Four factor theory of leadership: a smallest space analysis. *Research Bulletin*, no. 10, 1969. Ann Arbor: The University of Michigan, Center for Research on the Utilization of Scientific Knowledge.

Brewster, K. 1970. Commencement address given at Michigan State University and reported in *The Chronicle of Higher Education* vol. 4 (13).

Brown, D. R. 1968. Student stress and student development. *Memo to the Faculty*, no. 26, January, 1968. Ann Arbor: The University of Michigan, Center for Research on Learning and Teaching.

———. 1969. Emerging social problems: for which does higher education have special responsibility? What structural devices are needed to cope with them? Paper presented at the American Association for Higher Education 24th National Conference on Higher Education, March, 1969, Chicago, Illinois.

————. 1973. A survey of U-M teaching fellows. Unpublished report cited in *Memo to the Faculty*, no. 51, March, 1973. Ann Arbor: The University of Michigan, Center for Research on Learning and Teaching.

Brown, W. E. 1967. Increasing productivity and reducing disease. The dental health team: potential role of auxiliaries. *American Dental Association Journal* 75:882–86.

Carnegie Commission on Higher Education. 1972. *The fourth revolution*. Hightstown, N.J.: McGraw-Hill.

Carrington, P. D., ed. 1971. Training for the public professions of the law: 1971, p. 2. Association of American Law Schools, 1971 Annual Meeting.

Centra, J. A. 1972. Strategies for improving college teaching. American Association for Higher Education, ERIC Clearinghouse on Higher Education report, no. 8, 1972.

Commission on College Physics, 1971. *Newsletter*, no. 25, November, 1971. College Park, Md.: University of Maryland.

Costin, F. 1972. Lecturing versus other methods of teaching: a review of research. *British Journal of Educational Technology*, January, 1972, 1 (3):4–31.

Costin, F., Greenough, W. L., and Menges, R. J. 1971. Student ratings of college teaching: reliability, validity, and usefulness. *Review of Educational Research* 41 (5):511–35.

Course Mart. 1972. Abstract in Committee on Institutional Cooperation (CIC) Report, no. 8, 1972, pp. 31–32. The University of Michigan, Center for Research on Learning and Teaching, Ann Arbor, Michigan.

Crane, H. R. 1968. Students do not think physics is relevant. *American Journal of Physics* 36:1137.

Dewey, J. *How we think.* 1910, rev. ed. 1933. New York: Heath and Co.

Dressel, P. L., and Thompson, M. M. 1973. *Independent study.* San Francisco: Jossey-Bass.

Dubin, R., and Taveggia, T. C. 1968. *The teaching-learning paradox: A comparative analysis of college teaching methods.* Eugene: University of Oregon Press.

Ebel, R. L. 1973. The future of the measurement of abilities II. *Educational Researcher* 2 (3):5–12.

Egan, D. E., and Greeno, J. G. 1973. The knowledge basis for cognitive behavior. A symposium paper given May, 1973, at Carnegie-Mellon University, Pittsburgh, Pennsylvania.

Else, G. F., and Haney, J. E. 1972. The center for coordination of ancient and modern studies. *Research News,* March, 1972. Ann Arbor: The University of Michigan, Office of Research Administration.

Empire State College Annual Report. 1972. *Seeking alternatives.* Albany: State University of New York.

Ericksen, S. C. 1955. A terminal course for psychology majors. *The American Psychologist* 10:22–24.

————. 1973. Development and experiment in college teaching at the Big Ten universities. Panel on Research and Development of Instructional Resources (CIC) Report, no. 9. The University of Michigan, Center for Research on Learning and Teaching, Ann Arbor, Michigan.

Erikson, E. H. 1963. *Youth: change and challenge.* New York: Basic Books.

Estes, W. K. 1972. Reinforcement in human behavior, *American Scientist* 60 (6):723–29.

Fader, D. N., and Schaevitz, M. H. 1966. *Hooked on books.* New York: Berkeley.

Feldman, K. A., and Newcomb, T. M. 1969. *The impact of college on students.* San Francisco: Jossey-Bass.

Flanders, N. A. 1960. Diagnosing and using social structures in classroom learning. In *The dynamics of educational groups* National Society for the Study of Education Yearbook, 1960.

Fowler, J. 1969. Content and process of physics teaching. *American Journal of Physics* 37:1194–1200.

Fowler, T., ed. 1890. *Locke's conduct of the understanding.* Oxford: Clarendon.

Gardner, J. 1964. The flight from teaching. Annual Report 1963–64 of the Carnegie Foundation for the Advancement of Teaching.

Geis, G. L., and Pascal, C. E. 1970. Consequences of learning. *Learning and Development,* October, 1970. Montreal: McGill University, Centre for Learning and Development.

Glaser, R. 1972. Individuals and learning: the new aptitudes. *Educational Researcher* 1 (6):5–13.

Glucksberg, S., and Weisberg, R. W. 1966. Verbal behavior and problem solving: some effects of labeling in a functional fixedness problem. *Journal of Experimental Psychology* 71:659–64.

Goldschmid, M. L. 1971. The learning cell: an instructional innovation. *Learning and Development,* January, 1971. Montreal: McGill University, Centre for Learning and Development.

Gould, S. B., and Cross, K. P. 1972. *Explorations in non-traditional study.* San Francisco: Jossey-Bass.

Graubard, A. 1972. The free school movement. *Harvard Educational Review* 42 (3):351–73.

Greenbaum, L. A. 1970. The tradition of complaint. *College English*, November, 1970, p. 174.

Guilford, J. P. 1950. Creativity. *American Psychologist* 9:444–54.

———. 1959. Three faces of intellect. *American Psychologist* 14:469–79.

Hamilton, A. 1965. Here come the tutors. *PTA Magazine* 60:7–9.

Hammond, A. L. 1972. Computer-assisted instruction: two major demonstrations. *Science* 176 (4039):1110–12.

Harlow, H. F. 1949. The formation of learning sets. *Psychological Review* 56:51–65.

Hatch, D. D. 1972. The pilot program: a residential experiment for underclassmen. *Memo to the Faculty*, no. 47, January, 1972. Ann Arbor: The University of Michigan, Center for Research on Learning and Teaching.

Hechinger, F. 1973. Students of the sixties: salvaging the youth movement. *Change* 5 (5):31–35.

Hesse, H. 1931. *Narcissus and Goldmund.* New York: Bantam Books.

Hildebrand, M. 1972. How to recommend promotion for a mediocre teacher without actually lying. *The Journal of Higher Education*, 43 (1):44–62.

Hilgard, E. R. 1963. The human dimension in teaching. Paper presented at Faculty Fall Conference, September, 1963, Stephens College, Columbia, Missouri.

Holbrook, R. 1971. Simulation of a world economy. Panel on Research and Development of Instructional Resources (CIC) Report, no. 7, 1971. The University of Michigan, Center for Research on Learning and Teaching, Ann Arbor, Michigan.

Hoyt, D. P. 1965. The relationship between college grades and adult achievement: a review of the literature. *Research Reports*, no. 7. Iowa City: American College Testing Program. Quoted in *Memo to the Faculty*, no. 18, June, 1966. Ann Arbor: The University of Michigan, Center for Research on Learning and Teaching.

Humphries, L. G. 1968. The fleeting nature of the prediction of college academic success. *Journal of Educational Psychology* 59:375–80.

Judd, C. H. 1908. The relation of special training to general intelligence. *Educational Review* 36:28–42.

Katona, G. 1969. Four responses to the president's letter. *Memo to the Faculty*, no. 36, August, 1969. Ann Arbor: The University of Michigan, Center for Research on Learning and Teaching.

Keller, F. S. 1972. Cited in *Proceedings*, ed. A. J. Dessler. Keller Method Workshop Conference, March 18, 1972, at Rice University, Houston, Texas.

Koen, F. M. 1972. Effects of pass-fail grading in an introductory psychology course—1970–71. In-house report, The University of Michigan, Center for Research on Learning and Teaching, Ann Arbor, Michigan.

Koen, F. M., and Ericksen S. C. 1967. An analysis of the specific features which characterize the more successful programs for the recruitment and training of college teachers. The University of Michigan, Center for Research on Learning and Teaching, Ann Arbor, Michigan. (Office of Education, U.S. Department of Health, Education, and Welfare, Project No. S-482, Contract No. OE-6-10-227.)

Krathwohl, D., Bloom, B. S., and Masia, B., eds. 1964. *Taxonomy of educational objectives: Handbook II affective domain.* New York: David McKay.

Kulik, J. A. 1972. Keller-based plans for teaching and learning: a review of research. Unpublished manuscript, October, 1972. The University of Michigan, Center for Research on Learning and Teaching, Ann Arbor, Michigan.

———. 1973. *Undergraduate education in psychology.* Washington, D.C.: American Psychological Association.

Kulik, J. A., Kulik, C., and Carmichael, K. 1973. The Keller plan in science teaching. Unpublished research report, The University of Michigan, Center for Research on Learning and Teaching, Ann Arbor, Michigan.

Kumar, V. K. 1971. The structure of human memory and some educational implications. *Review of Educational Research* 41 (5):379–417.

Likert, R. 1961. *New patterns of management.* New York: McGraw-Hill.

MacLeish, A. 1972. The premise of meaning. *American Scholar* 41:357–62.

MacLeod, R. B. 1965. The teaching of psychology and the psychology we teach. *American Psychologist* 20:344–52.

Mager, R. F. 1962. *Preparing objectives for programmed instruction.* San Francisco: Fearon Publishers.

Maier, N. R. F. 1971. Innovation in education. *American Psychologist* 26:722–25.

Main, D. B., and Head, S. 1971. Computer simulations in the elementary psychology laboratory. Paper presented at the Conference on Computers in the Undergraduate Curricula, June 23–25, 1971, at Dartmouth College, Hanover, New Hampshire.

Maltzman, I. 1960. On the training of originality. *Psychological Review* 67:229–42.

Mann, R., Arnold, S. M., Binder, J., Cytrynbaum, S., Newman, B. M., Ringwald, B., Ringwald, J., and Rosenwein, R. 1970. *The college classroom: conflict, change, and learning.* New York: Wiley.

March, R. H. 1970. *Physics for poets.* New York: McGraw-Hill.

Maslow, A. H. 1970. Humanistic education vs. professional education: further comments. *New Directions in Teaching,* vol. 2 (2).

———. 1971. *The farther reaches of human nature.* New York: Viking.

Mayhew, L. B. 1971. Can undergraduate independent study courses succeed? *College Board Review* 79:26–30.

McKeachie, W. J. 1965. The discussion group. *Memo to the Faculty,* no. 14, November, 1965. Ann Arbor: The University of Michigan, Center for Research on Learning and Teaching.

———. 1971. Research on college teaching. *Memo to the Faculty,* no. 44, May, 1971. Ann Arbor: The University of Michigan, Center for Research on Learning and Teaching.

McKee, J. M. 1964. The Draper experiment: a programmed learning project. In *Trends in programmed instruction,* ed. G. D. Ofiesh and W. C. Meierhenry. Washington, D.C.: Department of Audiovisual Instruction, National Education Association.

———. 1971–73. Rehabilitation Research Foundation, Phase III, Final report, September, 1971 to February, 1973. Elmore, Alabama.

Mikulas, W. L. 1970. Interactions of attitudes and associative interference in classroom learning. *Journal of Experimental Education* 39 (2):49–55.

Miller, A. R. 1970. *The assault on privacy: computers, data banks, and dossiers.* Ann Arbor: The University of Michigan Press.

Miller, D. 1973. Follow-up evaluation of teaching fellows. Unpublished report cited in *Memo to the Faculty,* no. 51, March, 1973. Ann Arbor: The University of Michigan, Center for Research on Learning and Teaching.

Miller, D., and O'Connor, P. 1973. The faculty/research conflict. Unpublished report cited in *Memo to the Faculty,* no. 51, March, 1973. Ann Arbor: The University of Michigan, Center for Research on Learning and Teaching.

Miller, S. 1967. *Measure, number and weight: a polemical statement of the college grading problem.* Ann Arbor: The University of Michigan, Center for Research on Learning and Teaching.

Milton, O. 1972. *Alternatives to the traditional.* San Francisco: Jossey-Bass.

Morrisett, L., and Hovland, C. 1959. A comparison of three varieties of training in human problem solving. *Journal of Experimental Psychology* 58:52–55.

Newcomb, T. M. 1970. What happens to students in college? *Memo to the Faculty,* no. 41, June, 1970. Ann Arbor: The University of Michigan, Center for Research on Learning and Teaching.

Newcomb, T. M., Brown, D. R., Kulik, J. A., Reimer, D. J., and Revelle, W. R. 1971. The University of Michigan's Residential College. In *The new colleges: toward an appraisal,* ed. P. L. Dressel, pp. 99–141. Iowa City: American College Testing Program.

Newman, J. H. 1968. On the scope and nature of university education. Everyman's Library, 1949 reprint. Quoted in *Objectives in higher education,* R. M. Beard, F. G. Healey, and P. J. Holloway, 1968, p. 32. London: Society for Research into Higher Education Ltd.

O'Connor, P. 1964. Motivation to learn. *Memo to the Faculty,* no. 7, September, 1964. Ann Arbor: The University of Michigan, Center for Research on Learning and Teaching.

Pace, C. R. 1969. College and university environment scales (CUES), 2d ed. Princeton, N.J.: Educational Testing Service.

Pascal, C. E. 1967. Some preliminary data about the pass-fail option. *Memo to the Faculty,* no. 22, April, 1967. Ann Arbor: The University of Michigan, Center for Research on Learning and Teaching.

Quart, L., and Stacey, J. 1972. Innovation on Staten Island. *Change,* June, 1972, pp. 14–18.

Rajecki, D. W. 1972. *Exper Sim: Computer Simulations for Teaching Elementary Research Design in Psychology.* Ann Arbor: The University of Michigan, Center for Research on Learning and Teaching.

Roe, A. A. 1943. A psychological study of eminent psychologists and anthropologists, and a comparison with biological and physical scientists. *Psychological Monographs,* no. 352.

Rogers, C. 1967. The facilitation of significant learning. In *Instruction: some contemporary viewpoints,* ed. L. Siegel. San Francisco: Chandler.

———. 1969. *Freedom to learn.* Columbus, Ohio: Chas. E. Merrill.

Rogers, J. Behavioral objectives in the "survey" course. *Educational Technology,* in press.

Ross, W. D., ed. 1927. *Aristotle selections.* New York: Charles Scribner's Sons.

Roszak, T. 1969. *The making of a counter culture.* New York: Doubleday.

Rothkopf, E. Z. 1970. The concept of mathemagenic activities. *Review of Educational Research* 40:325–36.

Roueche, J. E., and Kirk, R. W. 1973. *Catching up: remedial education.* San Francisco: Jossey-Bass.

Rubino, V. J., ed. 1972. *Survey of clinical legal education 1971–72.* New York: Council on Legal Education for Professional Responsibility, Inc.

Sanford, N., ed. 1962. *The American College.* New York: John Wiley.

Skinner, B. F. 1948. *Walden two.* New York: Macmillan.

———. 1953. *Science and human behavior.* New York: Macmillan.

———. 1954. The science of learning and the art of teaching. *Harvard Educational Review* 24:86–97.

———. 1968. *The technology of teaching.* New York: Appleton-Century-Crofts.

———. 1971. *Beyond freedom and dignity.* New York: Knopf.

Spence, K. E. 1959. The relation of learning theory to the technology of education. *Harvard Educational Review* 29:84–95.

Sutherland, E., ed. 1965. *Letters from Mississippi.* New York: McGraw-Hill.

Szent-Gyorgyi, A. 1964. Teaching and the expanding knowledge. *Science* 146:1278–79.

Teske, R. G. 1972. Abstract cited in *Memo to the Faculty*, no. 50, December, 1972. Ann Arbor: The University of Michigan, Center for Research on Learning and Teaching.

Thorndike, E. L. 1911. *Animal intelligence.* New York: Macmillan. Cited in *Reinforcement and behavior*, H. C. Wilcoxon, 1969, pp. 12–13. New York: Academic Press.

Thornton, J. W., ed. 1972. *The laboratory: a place to investigate.* The Commission on Undergraduate Education in the Biological Sciences, publication no. 33, 1972.

Union for Experimenting Colleges and Universities. 1972. *University without walls.* Rev. ed. Antioch College, Yellow Springs, Ohio.

Warner, S. B., and Mann, J. B. 1972. Development of options in a history course. Abstract in Committee on Institutional Cooperation (CIC) report, no. 8, 1972, p. 15. Ann Arbor: The University of Michigan, Center for Research on Learning and Teaching.

Warren, J. R. 1970. College grading practices: an overview. Princeton, N.J.: Educational Testing Service.

————. 1971. Current grading practices. Research Report, no. 3, 1971. Washington, D.C. American Association for Higher Education.

White, R. W. 1959. Motivation reconsidered: the concept of competence. *Psychological Review* 26:360–73.

Williams, A. F. 1972. Abstract of a study cited in *Behavioral Sciences Newsletter for Research Planning* vol. 9 (22), prepared by the American Institutes for Research in the Behavioral Sciences.

Wood, C. 1972. A new German grammar. Panel on Research and Development of Instructional Resources (CIC) report, no. 8, 1972. Ann Arbor: The University of Michigan, Center for Research on Learning and Teaching.

Zinn, K. L. 1971. Requirements for programming languages in computer-based instructional systems. In *Educational Yearbook*, 1971–72, ed. A. Daniels. London: The British Computer Society.

Index